HAPPINESS EXPLAINED

PAUL ANAND

HAPPINESS
EXPLAINED

What human flourishing is and
what we can do to promote it

OXFORD
UNIVERSITY PRESS

OXFORD
UNIVERSITY PRESS

Great Clarendon Street, Oxford, OX2 6DP,
United Kingdom

Oxford University Press is a department of the University of Oxford.
It furthers the University's objective of excellence in research, scholarship,
and education by publishing worldwide. Oxford is a registered trade mark of
Oxford University Press in the UK and in certain other countries

© Paul Anand 2016

The moral rights of the author have been asserted

First Edition published in 2016

Impression: 1

Published in the United States of America by Oxford University Press
198 Madison Avenue, New York, NY 10016, United States of America

British Library Cataloguing in Publication Data

Data available

Library of Congress Control Number: 2015949395

ISBN 978-0-19-873545-8

Printed in Great Britain by
Clays Ltd, St Ives plc

For my family and the many friends and colleagues who have helped along the way, particularly Anne, John, Hon, and Tamsen.

PREFACE

In *Happiness Explained* I seek to show that, instead of focusing on money as our metric of progress, it is possible to 'go beyond GDP' by developing and analysing measures of human wellbeing. This is not to suggest we should forsake the material world or become Trappist monks but rather just to acknowledge the fact that there is, globally, growing interest in non-financial measures of life quality. For many who are comfortably off in financial terms, it seems a logical next step to ask whether material affluence is delivering the quality of life we seek, but success in the material realm is also having an effect on society's hopes for those less fortunate. And there is a range of questions that follow. Am I able to get the balance between family and work that I want? What do I need in terms of personal growth and development? Will I be able to find decent employment when I need to? What career path is best suited for my skills? How can I look after my family and care for those with whom I am connected by various bonds of duty and commitment? Given the diversity of issues involved, it should not be surprising to find that no particular science seems to have a monopoly of wisdom when it comes to happiness and wellbeing. For these reasons, therefore, I offer, here, a short guide to a vast territory of research from economics through psychology to philosophy that can help us think about happiness and wellbeing both at an individual level and in a societal context.

It is natural to ask, early on, what we mean by terms such as happiness or wellbeing and as it happens, both can be traced back to the ancient Greek stem 'eu' meaning 'well'. This root appears in words still used, such as eulogy (good words) and interest in it goes back to the ethical theory of eudaimonia (good spirit) developed by

Aristotle who argued for the importance of both internal personality characteristics as well as visible, external factors such as income or health. In Old French, *eu* became *heur* from which derives happy in English, a word that qualifies its subject (happy family, happy coincidence and so on) in much the same way as did its ancient Greek counterpart.

Happiness sometimes takes on a narrow meaning related to a person's state of mind and there is evidence of such use in English in the early sixteenth century though this narrow usage has never excluded the broader sense generally associated with wellbeing. The term 'human flourishing' is perhaps a reasonable modern counterpart to Aristotle's eudaimonia and I shall therefore occasionally use wellbeing and happiness to refer to external and internal issues recognizing that these are usually connected and often closely so.

In my own team's work, we have been interested in measuring human flourishing and using the resulting data to understand how wellbeing is produced and distributed. The field attracts its fair share of work on the technicalities of index design and our own research has included some such activity but here I want to focus on some more basic but equally important issues, namely what are the dimensions in which human wellbeing resides, what are the drivers or causes of wellbeing, and how do all of these change over the human life course? There have been those who thought that science should focus on things that are 'hard' and measurable and that happiness was neither, but the perspective no longer feels like the majority view it might once have been. At a population level, there *are* clearly some common patterns that tell us about the kinds of things that help life go well (or otherwise).

A number of sciences are contributing to our understanding of human wellbeing, though particularly evident are contributions from experimental and social psychology, empirical economic modelling, and ethics. Both psychology and economics have had longstanding interests in human wellbeing though it is arguably only in the past twenty years that this has been reflected in major research programmes such as those drawn on in Chapters 5 and 6. In part, science has been responding to global changes in the social world. Education, technological change, and increasing global trade have helped countries increase their national incomes in financial terms and this in turn has led to improved quality of life and aspirations for millions. And alongside this progress there have emerged a raft of new challenges of which rising inequality is one. Increasingly, it becomes easier to identify such difficulties—people can compare their own lot with that of others around the world using their computers, televisions, and phones in an instant.

Research and policy have become closely related in recent years. Novel methods, theories and technologies of measuring human happiness and wellbeing have been met with interest from political and business leaders keen to develop and exploit the practical implications and policy opportunities. Similarly in the social realm, a much wider range of social relations are supported in many countries than was the case fifty years ago. So it is against the background of this confluence of evidence, theory, and ideas on the one hand, and changing social and economic needs and wants on the other, that this book is set. Although not intended to be an academic book, it draws extensively on research. In particular, I spend some time explaining a new approach developed by a Nobel Laureate in Economics that I, and my colleagues, have sought to operationalize over the past decade and a half. When we started this work, there was a question as to whether the approach *could* be operationalized but I hope that our work has helped to encourage the realization that direct measurement is indeed possible and that the emerging questions are to do with use in analysis, policy, and practice. In addition, what I hope to show is that the ideas Sen first developed in the early 1980s have a structure and insight into human wellbeing that permit a strong connection to psychology, which is essential if the ethical and human rights-based concerns that people interested in human flourishing have are to be successfully implemented in the real world.

In the course of doing this work, I have become particularly interested in the capacity of the underlying formal framework to act as a kind of universal grammar for thinking about life quality. Compared with the utilitarian approach which dominated welfare economics for most of the last century, the current approach does not force us to take into account the pleasures of the sadist, assume that *only* money matters or is measurable, or that there is something suspect about being concerned about fairness. There has, in psychology, emerged a recent tendency to make a distinction between *hedonic* pleasures and *eudaimonic* wellbeing, and to equate the former with happiness measured by life satisfaction. I won't be following this line exactly because life satisfaction appears theoretically and in practice to be more of a reflective judgement than an expression of mood. Indeed there is an asymmetry between summary experiences and our judgements about the state of affairs. Even if people are satisfied with life, this does not mean that there aren't things that can be done to improve their wellbeing. And when focusing on experiential measures the purpose of science is to find what their drivers are and to do this we need an account of the dimensions of life quality that people value. We know quite a bit about this from early psychological research developed and reviewed by Michael Argyle, but the application of new techniques helps to make the point that experiential measures of happiness are explained by many different factors—hence the need for the multi-dimensional approach introduced particularly in Chapter 3. Even though measures such as life satisfaction are used now both by economists and psychologists, we shall also see that they tend to pick out personal and social issues clearly—though at the cost of external and non social factors—for example those to do with the physical environment, which can have significant impacts on other aspects of wellbeing, such as physical health. Against this background, our approach has been to develop new data on the different dimensions of life quality and then see what insights about the production and distribution of wellbeing can be derived from analysing such data.

There are various reasons why we should monitor human happiness and wellbeing without jumping to any conclusions about how it should best be promoted but perhaps one of the simplest justifications is a kind of 'evening up' argument. We measure and monitor millions of financial transactions that take place every day so why should we not also become more informed about the ultimate outcomes that these transactions are supposed to help us achieve? We know so much more about the means than the ends and the imbalance is such that some redress now seems in order.

Although I have tried to show how different scientific disciplines all make essential contributions to explaining personal wellbeing, I see economics as being particularly valuable for its scientific tools which can be used to integrate insights from psychology, mental health, and a range of other areas of science. Chapters 1, 2, and 3 particularly focus on understanding the explanatory framework while Chapters 4 through 8 use the concept of human flourishing to marshal evidence about some of the key drivers of happiness and wellbeing. My own research has focused on demonstrating the workability of this approach and how it provides an alternative to income accounting, as developed by economists such as Petty, Stone, Kuznets, and Frisch. The indicators considered here speak to both the subjective agenda pioneered by psychologists and economists, but also the so-called philosophical objective lists that have received less scientific attention until recently. Sir Isaiah Berlin, the philosopher and polymath, once wrote that the fox is content to know only many things while the hedgehog is frustrated by this and wants to know one big thing. He thought of himself as a fox but also proposed that there is something of both in all of us. In the realm of happiness and wellbeing, there are certainly very many things to be known but whether there is one big thing to know I leave for readers (and hedgehogs) to decide.

Paul Anand
Oxford
2016

TABLE OF CONTENTS

CHAPTER 1

THE NEED TO GO BEYOND GDP

Limits of GDP as a Measure of Human Wellbeing

The world monitors financial performance on a regular, if not obsessive, basis, and for most countries this is done by reporting the nation's gross domestic product (GDP). The process of national income accounting from which GDP is derived can be traced back to the work of Sir William Petty, a one-time Oxford astronomer who in the 1640s became interested in statistics and economics and estimated, for the first time, the national income of England to be something in the region of £40m. Three hundred years later, and based significantly on refinements of his work by notable figures including Sir Richard Stone, Simon Kuznets, and Ragnar Frisch, a global system of national accounting was introduced and it has held sway around the world for over three-quarters of a century.

As a result, we quantify progress and human wellbeing in terms of income. In 2012, for example, the GDP of the United States, per person, was US$51,749 while, for the United Kingdom, the figure was US$39,093. These figures make it sound as if people in the U.S. were significantly better off than their U.K. counterparts, but what exactly does a comparison of this sort really tell us?

In a nutshell, GDP is the market value of goods and services produced by a country in any one year. So the figures above suggest that, for each person on average, production in the U.S. was valued over 20 per cent more than that in the U.K. Does that mean human wellbeing in the U.S. was also over 20 per cent greater than in the U.K.? It is common sense to say that there must be some relation between income measured in financial terms and human wellbeing, and that people living in abject poverty will benefit significantly from higher incomes but beyond that, it is rather harder to determine precisely just how closely related human wellbeing and personal income actually are. For one thing, holiday entitlements are significantly less in the U.S. than they are in the U.K.; for another, access to healthcare does not depend on how much an adult earns in the U.K.; and on top of this, social (im)mobility is about the same in both countries—though people often believe it to be much greater in the U.S. So when one starts to add in these other aspects of welfare, the financial disparity does not seem to tell the full story.

For much of the twentieth century, economists would caution that measures of economic welfare are not good measures of human wellbeing before using them anyway in the absence of anything better. In recent years, however, a number of researchers and policy-makers have started to take the difficulty seriously and as a result there is now a consensus that human wellbeing should and can be measured directly and explicitly. There is even significant voter support for these initiatives. In a national consultation across the U.K., three-quarters of respondents believed that personal wellbeing should be monitored to inform and address the long-term challenges facing the promotion of human wellbeing.

In the main part of this book, I indicate how we might define 'wellbeing' and what research tells us about it, but for the sake of completeness, I want in this chapter, to spell out a bit more why economists and others view GDP as an insufficient yardstick for measuring wellbeing.

William Petty's underlying purpose was to contribute to a debate about the source of national wealth, which, according to a predominant view, was related to the accumulation of gold bullion. In fact, Petty claimed to show that some 80 per cent of the country's wealth was produced by the fruits of human labour, so while he is a founding father of financial measurement, he also made a point about the social nature of income production. Even if one valued only income (not a position I shall take here), the human contribution was essential. Empirical evidence in science generally needs a theoretical framework and Petty's proposal was one in which income was determined by money flowing around the economy, just as goods and services are traded between buyers and sellers. This circular flow model gives rise to some important predictions about the consequences of trade for the health of an economy and has contributed to thinking that exports and free trade are an important source of long-term global progress. In short, GDP is just one statistic from a system of national income measurement which has a significant history, some simple but valuable theory behind it, and gives governments and businesses a picture of where their economies and markets are going. It is no wonder that such accounts rolled out around the world during the first half of the twentieth century and perhaps only surprising that this did not happen sooner.

Despite the enormous intellectual and political achievements, national income accounts can be questioned in some important ways. Although national income may be a good measure of the value of business output, how good a measure is it of other things we value? Writing in 1974, Richard Easterlin was one of the first economists to draw attention to this question with a simple graph in which he showed that over a 20-year period, while U.S. income rose dramatically, satisfaction with life remained as flat as the proverbial pancake. If rising income is the means to improving life quality then why, Easterlin asked, in periods of robust economic growth, did satisfaction with life not follow the same trend?

There are several other reasons why we might not regard financial measures as adequate proxies of human wellbeing and here I want to mention three more. The first is nicely illustrated by the fact that some years ago, a well-known Oxford resident placed a large plastic shark on his roof, thus providing a visual impact that was positive or negative depending on the perspectives of neighbours and passers-by. In economic terms, such impacts are called externalities as they are not costed or valued in economic activity though they are associated with it.

Externalities in general derive from over- or under-production of goods and services, and can be widespread. One of the first examples used to make the point concerned the location of factories in residential areas: industrial activity can create noise or air pollution that has a negative impact on people; it arises from economic activity but typically factory owners do not compensate their surrounding neighbours for the losses they suffer as a result. Economic growth, traditionally defined, generates a range of such externalities from climate change through to criminal behaviour. If a natural resource is spoiled, there is no mechanism for recording the loss, as the national accounts only record income flows and not the values of assets. In short, there are many things that matter and are of value to us not reflected in any of the standard financial measures of income.

A second set of issues concerns what goes on inside families. Arthur Pigou made the point by noting that someone could marry their housekeeper and thereby reduce national income without changing any of the activities that were undertaken. While the example is in some ways dated, its importance remains as much time is spent doing unpaid work inside the home—caring for children, the elderly, the sick, and performing a range of household chores. Currently these activities are not part of the national accounts though they would be if we paid others to do them for us, as is increasingly the case. But is it always a good thing that household activities be farmed out to people we pay? Does everything have to be paid for in a market transaction in order to be recognized as being valuable? The answers to these questions are far from obvious.

Finally, a third issue concerns inequalities, which have been discussed most recently by the economist, Thomas Piketty. Traditionally, national income is reported as an average per person, though actual individual incomes vary hugely. Economists have become increasingly interested in the distribution of income and wealth in recent decades and typically use a measure called the Gini coefficient to measure inequality. Income growth is supposed to alleviate poverty but if the income distribution becomes more unequal, then those not at the top may in relative terms feel worse off. In short, average national income isn't enough—it doesn't correspond to the relative and distributional concerns that shape most people's experience of how well they are doing.

These considerations, and there are several others, help to illustrate why national income is at best only a narrow indicator of progress. It is a good measure of the market value of corporate output, which explains why it features in the business sections of daily newspapers, and it measures welfare in terms of the value of corporate output. However, if we are concerned about welfare from economic activity in general, or the quality of our lives beyond the financial aspects, national income is limited. From a scientific perspective, the measurement of human wellbeing needs additional empirical information with a relevant theoretical underpinning. GDP and national income accounts are based on a theory that shows how income is determined but if we are interested in human wellbeing, then what we need is a different kind of theory, one that provides an account of what wellbeing and happiness are, and how they are produced and distributed.

As we shall see, such an account, initiated by Nobel prize-winner Amartya Sen, does indeed exist and in what follows I show that it can be used to provide a general approach to the measurement and understanding of human wellbeing. Indeed it can be used to identify aspects of wellbeing and happiness that fill the informational gaps left by income, though in general there is no single index we can use to replace GDP. For some, if not many purposes, the diverse aspects of wellbeing are, like apples and pears, too different to be usefully summed up in a single number. Nonetheless, if different aspects of life quality can be quantified in some way, then we can at least build models that help us understand the key drivers of human wellbeing, even if we can't have a perfect index.

Criteria for Indicators

If we are to develop an assessment of progress based on a set of measures or indicators of different aspects of life quality, certain criteria need to be considered. For one thing, scientific adequacy and practical usefulness are not necessarily the same thing: criteria and methods for good science can, in many areas, be specified in advance, whereas usefulness only emerges from serious attempts at application, often involving significant trial and error. In the world of measurement, we prize accuracy. No empirical measures are perfectly accurate but they need to be accurate enough for the purposes to which they are put. In addition, we want something that is a *valid* measure of the thing we want to quantify. Validity of new measures is often considered explicitly in health and psychology and the main point—not rocket science at a conceptual level—is that an indicator must relate closely to the thing you are trying to measure. There is a large literature, for example, on the measurement of health but what should this include? Can we have a measure of health that focuses just on physical functioning? What about pain or stress? Should these not also be included?

Such questions naturally lead on to an additional consideration when developing a set of indicators, namely the issue of *comprehensiveness*. If you are driving a car, you don't need to know everything about the car's performance at any point in time though there are a few things—speed, fuel, temperature, oil, and water—that you must be able to monitor. And you need to monitor them separately—it would not be much help if the manufacturer provided you with a single index number summarizing all the five variables. However simple and elegant this might be, it would also be completely meaningless. To drive the car, there are a few things that you need to know, and so it is with the alternatives to GDP for measuring quality of life. Everyone loves a good index and any set of numbers can be used to create one, but to monitor and understand quality of life we also need a well-chosen dashboard of indicators covering some quite diverse phenomena as we shall see in the chapters that follow.

It is often suggested, in addition, that indicators should be *decision-relevant*. Potentially, they might help governments allocate budgets within or between different departments and they are certainly used to allocate resources between geographical regions. Such allocations clearly have an impact on the quality of peoples' lives but the technicalities are such that they are often not as widely discussed or scrutinized as their implications warrant. Measuring different aspects of life quality holds out the prospect of being able to identify areas where there are problems, something that might not show up if we just focused on a single figure, such as GDP.

For indicators to be useful they need to be protected from manipulation by unscrupulous actors and there are a couple of ways in which the concern might apply to quality of life indicators. One concerns the fact is that when indicators paint a gloomy picture, politicians will seek to modify the ways variables are measured and there is some evidence from changes in measures of unemployment that suggests this can, indeed, be a genuine concern. A second worry seems to be that political actors will somehow try to manipulate the actual levels of population wellbeing and happiness. Of course it is wise to becautious about the interests of political actors but surely one of the things voters want is that they do respond to the full range of concerns about human wellbeing and not just issues backed by well-organized lobby groups.

Economists distinguish indicators of process from those of final outcomes though it can be a difficult distinction for public sector organizations to make in practice. Expenditure figures certainly measure activity and are usually easy to obtain but they say little in themselves as to whether an activity has produced great outcomes or white elephants. The point goes to the heart of why countries are interested in measures of wellbeing: for most people income is the means to diverse and valued ends and without a measure of the ends, we can have no way of gauging how effective the means are.

Research into the development of indicators suggests that participation in the construction fosters acceptance and use. Participation not only generates a sense of ownership, but is also likely to develop indicators more finely tuned to what is required. The U.K. government has consulted over 30,000 members of the public directly in its work on this area and the consultation provides valuable evidence of what citizens want.

Identifying the Wellbeing Space

In moving beyond income to a dashboard of indicators covering different aspects of life quality, a, if not the, key question concerns the space in which human wellbeing resides and is produced. What are the factors that cause life to go well, or sometimes trip us up? What are the particular aspects of the states we choose or find ourselves in that cause us to judge them good or bad? How should we think about the wellbeing consequences of everyday activities and the less visible opportunities that are essential for these activities to take place? In principle, these are simple questions and it is surprising, in a way, that economics has no standard answers to them—given the importance it attributes to consumer and personal freedom. Were one willing to grant that income is perfectly or even very closely related to human wellbeing in all matters, then perhaps understanding the space in which wellbeing is produced is merely a matter of scientific interest. However, if we find that the quality of life of people in old age, say, has very little to do with current changes in GDP, and if we are interested in wellbeing during that phase of life, then we have good reason to find out what does, in fact, drive wellbeing at that stage in life.

So how might we investigate the space in which human wellbeing exists? There have been many attempts to do this from philosophical, religious, and legal perspectives and the current approach's emphasis on multiple dimensions provides the necessary framework for doing this empirically. What really matters to us? What affects the objective conditions in which we live, and what drives our personal experiences of life? And how different are we in these regards? These are some of the central questions of wellbeing and happiness our approach is designed to address.

Many accounts of the dimensions and drivers of happiness and wellbeing have been categorized as 'objective lists', as they specify a series of things believed to be good for individuals and societies. The term 'objective' can be a bit misleading as the common theme in such lists is the promotion of human wellbeing rather than any particular claim to objectivity. It is the near universal agreement that matters and in some cases—for example, thou shalt not kill—such agreement is plausible and attractive. Indeed, despite important and interesting conceptual differences, these objective list accounts share, for the purposes of structuring empirical work, a lot of common ground. For that reason, we chose to draw particularly on a relatively broad list produced by political theorist, Martha Nussbaum, which in turn relates closely to principles articulated by the institutions of the United Nations as well as philosophical ideas propounded by Aristotle and John Rawls. We don't make or need to make claims that the list is universally correct for all democracies but have evolved an approach in which we do claim to have a dashboard of wellbeing indicators that sustain some useful analysis. Perhaps most important of all is the fact that we have consulted with some four to five thousand people in various ways across several studies in an attempt to find out what it is that matters to them. Understanding wellbeing depends, as I shall try to suggest, on combining inputs from the public, relevant scientific research, as well as views and theories about what people in some situations *should* do. Although, this book is primarily about marshalling evidence and considering some novel findings, a good theoretical framework is essential and in Chapter 2 we look at the human flourishing approach, developed within economics and increasingly of influence within psychology, as a basis for making sense of some of the evidence.

HUMAN FLOURISHING

If we are to evaluate progress, not just in financial terms but also in terms of human wellbeing and happiness, we need a framework that goes beyond the determinants of national income and engages with these human outcomes and their causes. This chapter outlines such a framework which provides a structure for monitoring and understanding the human outcomes of progress directly and explicitly. The framework was developed with its own technical language, though for the most part I use here everyday counterparts and draw on the mathematical structure only implicitly: the term 'human flourishing' has been used to refer to the overall framework and as it seems to have garnered some support in various places, I shall use it here.

Those who emphasize human flourishing often refer back to the Aristotelean origins of the concept and are typically concerned about the diversity of human potential and need as well as the promotion of both on an inclusive basis. Economics concentrates on the technical formulation of these issues and in doing so it often seems overly abstract to non-economists, but ideas once formalized can often be helpful even in a qualitative sense, as we shall see. Economists often prize generality and human flourishing is no exception as it offers a relatively *universal grammar* for understanding components of human wellbeing in the sense that it could equally be applied to understanding wellbeing in a small tribal group of people living hundreds of thousands of years ago, as it could to people living in the most advanced capitalist society today. So what exactly does this framework emphasize?

Activity, Experience and Opportunity

Human flourishing encourages us to think about the ultimate wellbeing outcomes we wish to pursue and achieve. A simple starting point might be to reflect on some of the things you did yesterday, and how you did them. Perhaps the things that come to mind are routine or time-consuming activities such as getting up, having breakfast, going to work, looking after children, doing some shopping. Maybe you did something more exotic like going out for a meal with friends. Perhaps you finished writing an essay or a report, or maybe you started to read a novel. In many if not most cases, activities are connected to a social role (family member, worker, student, and so on) and these roles contribute significantly to our personal identity and self-esteem. So together, what we do and who we are, are integral to wellbeing and happiness from day to day.

If you think back again to yesterday but focus this time on your experiences, you might well have felt any number of sensations or emotions. Perhaps it was a quiet day, or maybe there were things that made you smile, pleased you or gave you reason to be proud. Perhaps it was one that never quite got going or seemed to be full of minor irritations and frustration. Perhaps you were disappointed because your football team lost a game or you felt a 'warm glow' because someone thanked you for something you did for them. Even if we find it difficult to quantify and sum up these different experiences precisely, they are real enough to be things we regularly discuss with others (women a bit more than men according to evidence). Some people are concerned that data on quality of life should deal with hard, objective facts, but from an evolutionary perspective, experiences, by virtue of being pleasant or otherwise, help us know what is good and worth pursuing or bad and worth avoiding. How we feel about things, whether they are good for us or not, is something that cannot be ignored as any successful politician will confirm.

Taken together, activity and experience are integral to human well-being on a day-to-day level but there is, in addition, a range of potential concepts to do with opportunities, freedoms, constraints, and risks that also impact on life quality. You might value having had a phone with you on a journey you made yesterday in case something went wrong—however, the fact that you didn't have to use it doesn't mean you think taking it was a mistake. You might stay in your house at night because it would be less safe to walk about the local neighbourhood alone at that time. You might be studying for a degree that will transform your opportunities in terms of the jobs that you could reasonably apply for. You may have children whose values and skills you plan to help to develop over many years. And so on. The opportunities that we have and that we create for ourselves may be difficult to assess, as opportunities are typically not things we directly observe. However, the fact that we are willing to invest huge amounts of time, effort, and resource into their development suggests they are things that we can value highly as stepping stones to desirable activities and experiences.

So the argument, according to the theory of human flourishing, is that what we are free and able to do, what we actually do, and our experiences are all important contributions to our overall happiness (in the broad sense). This represents within economics something of a departure from the standard ways of thinking which, over the past century, have placed the focus fairly and squarely on income as the pathway to improvements in human wellbeing. Insufficient income, generally defined as relative to others in society, is seen as the marker of poverty which growth, it is hoped, will help reduce. According to this framework, however, income is an input into the development of valued outcomes, rather than their measure. Typically, income will be positively correlated with wellbeing and happiness but this is not always so and even when it is, we may need or wish to know much more if we are to understand or improve the production of human wellbeing.

The human flourishing approach views resources such as income as an input to the production of activities, and thereby experience, but doesn't assume the connection must always be through the consumption of goods and services. Furthermore, it doesn't assume that we can all convert financial resources into things we have reason to value at the same rate. People have very different capacities for converting income and other resources into valued activities and experiences so we shall need to look, not just at personal or even household income, but also at what a person can achieve, given their resources and skills. Moreover, even if we allow for different resources and skills, people will typically differ in how they experience particular activities. All of these considerations are allowed for and emphasized by our framework.

In a number of cases relating particularly to employment, public service, and education, we are interested to know whether a person has been afforded good or equitable opportunities to do the things that are generally valued in that society. Many countries, for example, protect the right for all to be treated equally in the workplace but we cannot, in general, check compliance just by looking at the work a person is doing or even by asking them how happy they feel. Rather, we shall need ways of investigating more directly the things they are able to do, as well as what they actually do and experience.

In principle then, we have a rich framework both for assessing quality of life and how resources and skills contribute to its production. If we want to provide an assessment of a person's wellbeing from an outcome perspective, we can enquire about their activities, experiences, and opportunities and in general, this will give something rather different to income, whether measured at the personal or national level. These are the core ideas—to understand a person's wellbeing we need to understand their opportunities, activities, and experiences, and to understand how these are produced in society we need to look at the role of resources and a range of personal factors. The chapters that follow show how this framework can be used but I want to conclude this discussion with comments about experience and resources, given their centrality in psychology and economics respectively.

Measures of Experience

Following the writings of the philosopher and economist, Jeremy Bentham, economists have focused on the concept of utility as the focal point for their analyses. The term happiness, sometimes used as a synonym for utility, can refer to experiences such as moods, which are rather private affairs and have little substantive claim on decisions about what a society should do (except perhaps through the ballot box). Sometimes people are asked questions about how happy they felt yesterday, for example, and such questions tap into that aspect of their experience. However, the concept of utility often has a more reflective and rational sense in economic analysis, one that resonates more closely with questions about how satisfied people feel with their lives overall. Questions along these lines have been used in psychology for a long time and analysed by economists significantly for at least a couple of decades. The resulting analyses are frequently referred to as 'happiness equations' though the variable often analysed, life satisfaction, is much closer in meaning to the more reflective, summative evaluation of life in the round. As a result, answers to questions about life satisfaction are plausible candidates for an overall summary measure of experience and perhaps as a result have been used widely by economists in recent years (as we shall see particularly in Chapter 5).

In the U.K., reflecting these considerations, the Office of National Statistics now asks people about their experience directly using four questions. In the first place, they are asked how satisfied they are with their life nowadays—essentially the long-standing psychological question increasingly used in economic analysis. In addition, there are two questions about how a person felt yesterday—worded in similar ways with the exception that the first refers to happiness and the second to anxiety. Finally, people are asked a question about the extent to which they feel the things they do in life are worthwhile. This question supposedly concerns the extent to which people derive meaning and purpose from the activities in which they choose to engage.

These experiential questions add to the dimensional evaluations above, based on what people can do. Such measures can be used for a variety of purposes including the identification of issues or groups where experience is poor. While happiness is strongly related to personal traits and skills that are relatively fixed for adults, the greater responsiveness of negative affect to external circumstances arguably makes it a better candidate as a diagnostic tool in policy or therapeutic contexts.

Resources

To bring about the life quality outcomes that we desire clearly requires resources. Thus far, we have assumed implicitly that such resources are financial and this might be enough for some purposes. For example, in debates about global inequality, it *might* be sufficient to make the main points about inequalities using data on the distribution of income and wealth around the world. It is more likely that this is all we can do given the data that is currently available for countries. However, there is no reason within this framework why we should not consider other kinds of resources. If, for example, we are interested in human wellbeing and happiness as an outcome, then it is natural to think that social as well as financial resources will be relevant. Indeed it is customary in this area to distinguish four different kinds of resources: financial, natural, human, and social. Financial resources involve income and wealth whereas natural resources refer to items in the physical environment as well as the services that can be derived from such environments.

The last two resource types are, by contrast, human in nature and refer respectively to a person's own assets and the community assets to which we all have access. Human capital relates to a person's knowledge and skills and is typically measured using formal qualifications. This leaves social resources, which are less often considered in economic analysis but are arguably essential when it comes to the production of happiness and wellbeing. When such resources are discussed, the concept of social capital has come to the fore so in this section, I want to consider the contribution that such resources might make.

Perhaps the first point to note is that if we are concerned about the mechanisms by which people achieve their own life quality, or the kinds of societies we wish to foster, then we need to recognize that a variety of social factors, such as norms, behaviours, and social ties do make a significant contribution to how wellbeing is produced and distributed. Furthermore, these social factors or resources obey different rules to those that govern their financial resources. Two definitions of social capital help make the point. One proposes that social capital is associated with the social structures that facilitate choices affecting more than one individual. An alternative definition focuses on the social, political, and economic environment that enable norms to develop which in turn shape the social structure. In both cases, the implication is that social resources will impact the opportunities that people have as a result of the social setting in which they find themselves. Social norms can certainly have a strong influence on the activities that people undertake but equally they might be so internalized that they ordinarily have little impact on the evaluative measures of experience discussed above, unless the norms happen to be violated.

As social norms and connections vary between individuals, it is natural to ask how much social capital any individual has. This latter idea is emphasized in the work of two sociologists who make a distinction between individual social capital in terms of personal contacts who might be in a position to provide help, and community social capital which is, in effect, the social quality of the environment in which a person lives, and is owned by all. The kinds of people we know, and the extent to which they might be in a position to provide help if needed, cannot be gleaned immediately from looking at a person's income, but these are factors that may well contribute to a person's wellbeing in adverse circumstances.

Another much considered feature of social resources concerns trust. One view about its value is simply that a society with lower levels of distrust will have fewer negative social interactions, lower transactions costs and thereby provide people with more opportunities to collaborate, and better experiences resulting from attempts to do so. Countries gripped by significant internal conflicts provide dramatic examples of how costly and disruptive the absence of trust can be but there are also questions, which seem unresolved at present, about the level and nature of trust in ordinary societies. Is trust declining? How do modern technologies hinder or facilitate the use and creation of trust within a society?

Viewed, potentially, as a major determinant of transactions costs, there is a concern that a decline in trust will cause legal costs to escalate. By contrast, transactions costs might be reduced significantly if, for example, the development of a shared identity can be created between people, something that Japanese car manufacturers were apparently able to successfully make use of many years through systems of company identity and loyalty. In any case, there is a growing recognition of the way in which social resources can impact quality of life at all levels within a society.

Skills

The social resources that you have access to not only depend on social structures but also on your talents and skills. Human flourishing emphasizes not only life quality outcomes but also the fact that people differ in their abilities to convert resources into valued outcomes. Traditionally, educational attainment has been the main measure of skill though it is commonplace to come across examples where the performance and contribution of people defy what might be expected by an examination of their academic records. The focus on educational records is somewhat pragmatic and reflects the availability of such data. It is, for example, recognized that tacit knowledge—perhaps gained through experience rather than formal training—can contribute to a person's productivity in the workplace. Similarly there is every reason to think that such non-academic skills may also contribute to the quality of a person's life though relevant data is harder to come by. Such skills are now often referred to as non-cognitive or soft skills, though neither term is terribly satisfactory. If these attributes are skills then presumably there must be some element of learning involved so they would seem to be cognitive after all. Furthermore, if there are identifiable, hard-won skills that have an impact on the outcomes which matter to us, then in what sense are they soft?

Putting It All Together

The elements above have a well-defined conceptual connection and can be used to generate empirical insights into the production and distribution of wellbeing *if* we have the right evidence. With appropriate data, we can monitor the different elements that contribute to life quality and we can begin to understand how resources and different kinds of skills contribute to their production. The resulting analyses might well enhance the workings of corporations but here I am mainly interested in developing a better understanding of life quality. Putting these ideas together empirically requires some specialist modelling, but there are potentially many insights that result and can be applied in everyday settings.

The relative contributions of resources and skills to a person's happiness will vary significantly for different aspects of areas of life. In any case, opportunities are particularly important for assessments of justice, as societies increasingly recognize that people can legitimately have very different tastes and preferences, and at the same time that opportunities to access valued social positions or core services should be equal between people. The second key relationship concerns the fact that day-to-day activities also depend on resources and skills though the contributions can vary dramatically between individuals. This is as true for the writing of a novel as it is for the raising of a family.

Finally, our framework suggests that experience depends on our activities and states. This seems to be a reasonable starting approximation and it allows for the fact that people will vary in how they experience the same activities. Indeed this view has been exploited in a piece of research by the psychologist Daniel Kahneman and colleagues who combined data on how people use their time, with experiential ratings of activity to calculate, for a sample of women from Texas in 2003, a measure of their happiness over a day. Their idea was that experienced wellbeing was a function of the activities engaged in, weighted by the amount of time spent in those activities. This relation between activities and experiential aspects of happiness is found in Sen's earlier account of human flourishing so there is clearly some agreement about the importance of activities, experience, and their connection.

There are then three basic facets of wellbeing, each of which depends on resources and skills. The three relations are particularly well suited to economic analysis because they provide ways of looking at production and distribution and the novelty is in looking at them directly rather than through a financial lens.

The Human Development Index

Human flourishing has already been highly influential in research and policy concerning lower income countries. More specifically, it has inspired the creation of the Human Development Index (HDI) calculated and published every year by the United Nations Development Program in its annual report. There has been much debate about the HDI even within proponents of the current framework, mainly on the grounds that it is a rather simple affair, comprising three equally weighted variables relating to average national income, life expectancy, and a country's overall literacy rate. Even this basic index has been a remarkable success in terms of focusing attention on the basic factors that matter for human flourishing and global progress. Health and education contribute not just to workforce productivity but also the full range of activities, opportunities, and experiences that people seek in fulfilling human lives.

Though calculated for most countries in the world, the HDI has been particularly influential in development circles where there was a frustration with development plans that took insufficient account of wellbeing outcomes like health, education, and the distribution of economic benefits within societies. It used to be assumed that, even if economic growth benefited the rich first and foremost, such benefits would trickle down to the poor though often such trickles were miniscule. By including health and education explicitly, the HDI has helped direct attention towards different routes and areas where life quality might be improved. As a result, new evidence concerning children, parents, and households has been developed and many countries have produced their own human development reports to shape national priorities and policies.

Perhaps the main limitation of this index, and its subsequent refinements, is that many high-income countries score relatively close to the top though the differences between them would be easier to discern if more aspects of wellbeing were measured. Chapter 3 illustrates, in effect, how the HDI can be extended significantly using data from the U.S. and U.K.

THE WELLBEING SPACE — WHAT IT IS AND HOW ARE WE DOING?

What People Are Able To Do

The most novel features of the human flourishing framework are that it focuses both on the opportunities and constraints that people face and emphasizes the many different dimensions of what people are free to do. In this chapter I draw particularly on research in which we have sought to operationalize this idea to thereby learn something about the structure of human wellbeing in an international setting.

In early research, we noted that there is a connection between opportunity and experience implied by the framework. If better opportunities allow people to engage in a wider set of activities, their measured experiences may well benefit as a result and our results appeared to confirm this connection. Indeed, when we model the possible drivers of life satisfaction we find a large number of very different kinds of factors are relevant. These include, for example, items such as quality of housing (for women), issues to do with being able to plan life as you would like, affording to go on holiday for a week, using talents and skills at work (for men), and, also at work, not being discriminated against. Results of a U.S.A.–U.K. comparison (from 1000 working-age adults in each country) are presented in Table 1 which reports average rankings of what people are able to do in the home, at work, in the community, the physical environment, and in terms of access to services. The data summarized here were collected by us with the aid of an opinion polling company, YOUGOV, in 2012 and to allow for the possibility that cultural factors might cause responses in one country to be higher than another, we compared the rankings within each country. The choice of items investigated draws on a variety of sources including our own previous research as well as similar exercises by government agencies and theoretical accounts developed by philosophers and social scientists.

Table 1: What People Are Able to Do

	U.S.	U.K.
Get my rubbish cleared away	1st	4th
Practise my religious beliefs	2nd	3rd
Make use of banking and personal finance services	3rd	1st
Keep a pet or animal at home with ease if I so wish	4th	8th
Get to a range of shops	5th	2nd
Get help from the police	6th	11th
Be treated where I live as an equal (and not discriminated against)	7th	9th
Express my political views when I wish	8th	7th
Get to places I need to without difficulty	9th	10th
Visit parks or countryside whenever I want	10th	5th
Be treated by a doctor or nurse	11th	6th
Walk in my local neighbourhood safely at night	12th	14th
Be treated as an equal (and not discriminated against) by people at work	13th	13th
Get trades people or the landlord to help fix problems in the house	14th	15th
Use my talents and skills at work	15th	17th

Find work when I need to	16th	18th
Socialize with others in family as I would wish	17th	19th
Find a home suitable for my needs	18th	16th
Feel valued and loved	19th	21st
Work under a good manager at the moment	20th	24th
Socialize at work	21st	27th
Fairly share domestic tasks with the household	22nd	23rd
Enjoy the kinds of personal relationships that I want	23rd	22nd
Make ends meet	24th	20th
Work in an environment that has little pollution	25th	25th
Get help from a solicitor	26th	12th
Achieve a good work–life balance	27th	26th
Take part in local social events	28th	28th
Be promoted or recognized at work	29th	29th

It is interesting to note that after 250 years of independence, inhabitants of one of the most technologically advanced societies in the world rank highest their ability to get their rubbish cleared away. This might seem curious until we recognize that the picture is little different in the U.K. where many of the other rankings are also rather similar. So perhaps it would seem that structural features of economies are playing a significant role in determining how this aspect of wellbeing is produced. In any case, this humble service is not as complex as many others though it is essential for public health and if things were to go wrong, it would not generally be difficult to identify the local political representatives ultimately responsible. Effective political accountability and competition may, therefore, be a contributory factor, and consistent with this is the finding that in Italy, where political tenure tends to be more short-lived and accountability harder to establish as a result, the ability to get rubbish cleared away is ranked much lower.

As we move down the table, the differences between the U.S. and U.K. tend to look rather modest though there are a few exceptions. Americans tend to rank more highly their ability to get help from the police whereas U.K. respondents appear to be more able to obtain medical assistance. Such findings are consistent with different policies and institutions for the provision of health but also with cultural and political differences about the balance between individual autonomy and the contribution that institutions necessarily make to problems that can only be solved at a collective level.

The fact that Americans would rank being able to socialize at work more highly was not obvious before we looked at the data. Perhaps it reflects traditional British reserve but another possibility is that such norms of behaviour are sensitive to incentives and that the relatively rapid hire-and-fire procedures which apply in the U.S. give people a stronger incentive to socialize at work. This could well be a good thing though job insecurity is generally a source of anxiety and ill-being so there are potentially swings and roundabouts here. Typically hire-and-fire rules and policies are evaluated in terms of their impact on corporate performance but the impact on human wellbeing may also be material even if not so obvious.

Towards the bottom of the list, in both countries, are the abilities to achieve a good work–life balance, take part in social events, and be promoted or recognized at work. Could it be that people just don't place much weight on these things? Local events, even when import- ant to people, can be infrequent and so not a major part of day-to-day life, but surely many people want a reasonable balance between the demands of work and all their other activities? There seems to be no simple explanation as to why its achievement comes so low in the table particularly given the fact it reflects the personal choices that people make. Perhaps people don't value this as much as they might think, or perhaps it is something that employers find costly to provide for workers. If a poor work–life balance has negative impacts on child development, as well as personal experience, then it would be seem to be good reason to try to understand in more detail what is going on here.

Work and Job Satisfaction

The low rating of promotion and recognition prospects in this list helps to raise the fact that work can play a crucial role in the quality of people's lives—and not just as a source of income. Harvard scholar Richard Freeman was one of the first to argue that economists should study job satisfaction and there is now a vast body of research on the topic. Originally developed by organizational psychologists to help corporations create more efficient working environments, the research is increasingly of interest to a range of individuals and organizations interested in trying to understand the factors that make work decent. There are, in fact, many such factors and fairness is clearly one of them. A large number of countries now espouse, in law at least, the idea that people should be treated equally, fairly, and without arbitrary discrimination though there is no global agreement as to what precisely equal treatment entails or how far it should be extended. That said, politicians who oppose equality in many countries often discover to their cost at the ballot box one of the reasons why equal treatment of men and women has taken hold.

In practice the implementation of equal opportunity principles is not always perfect and one explanation can be found in a hypothesis formulated by Gary Becker, which argues that companies will discriminate (unreasonably) between workers less as market conditions become *more competitive*. His idea is just that under competitive market conditions companies simply cannot afford the luxury of the wasted talent to which discrimination gives rise and it is not difficult to find evidence to support his theory.

Of course fairness is only one aspect of decent work as attempts to measure quality of life in the round indicate. An exercise by a

European think tank proposes the use of some eighty different indicators to monitor issues under four categories: career and employment security, health and wellbeing, skills development, and work–life balance. Specific issues include exposure to hazards, working hours, pace and intensity of work, violence in the work place, opportunities for participation and consultation, and there are no doubt other items that could be added. These indicators emphasize the things employers must promote (safety, for example) but there are other issues that can also often improve job satisfaction. It has been shown, for example, that the abilities to schedule tasks for ourselves and to make decisions about the way work is done are connected both to work satisfaction and productivity. Various aspects of task design including variety, significance, and the opportunity to use skills, are also valued by workers: tasks that are insufficiently demanding can lead to disengagement and boredom while those that are overly challenging generate stress.

The scope to process information and the opportunity to solve problems can also be sources of satisfaction at work and in some contexts there is an overlap with social sources of job satisfaction. Constructive feedback appropriately handled and social support from colleagues, for instance, can contribute to positive experiences of work, while the quality of immediate line management is often one of the main determinants of staff retention and job satisfaction. On the downside, roles that are not clearly defined or that are in conflict with others can be a source of dissatisfaction and contribute to life quality through anxiety, stress, exhaustion, and overload. The key themes seem to be autonomy, income stability, the suitability of tasks, the social quality of the managerial regime, and the fairness of the environment in which a person works. Where these are visible and the costs of losing trained staff are high, market forces can surely be relied upon to produce decent jobs but where these conditions don't hold, for example, for those in the least productive jobs, quality of life might depend on the nature of governmental policies as much as the presence of competition.

Aspects of Family Life

In the data from which the rankings above are drawn, it is noticeable that home-related capabilities are a significant source of variation in experiential assessments of quality of life. Home units are smaller than firms or communities so this is to be expected (statistically) but this also reflects the greater levels of societal and economic regulation that take place outside the personal private sphere in which household life takes place. The factors that drive happiness and wellbeing within the home are numerous and so to illustrate some of the issues, and the extent to which they are closely related to income or not, we consider some of the evidence concerning three illustrative issues, namely marital unions, offspring, and domestic violence.

Marital quality has been quantified in terms of a number of positive and negative aspects including satisfaction, commitment, support, interaction, forgiveness, and discord. Psychologists have commented on the way research has focused on difficulties and problems (the so-called deficit model) though it has been suggested that, for marriages in the U.S., about 80 per cent are either medium or high in terms of marital happiness and stay that way over a long period of time. A wide range of factors have been linked to the high marital quality group including being white, having fewer children and, perhaps a little curiously, wives working extended hours. Cohabiting raises the probability of being in the middle happiness group while marrying at a later age is associated with being in the lowest marital happiness group. Further, it has been found that husbands doing a greater proportion of housework or reporting equal decision-making were more likely to be in the high marital happiness group—as were those who reported greater beliefs in lifelong marriage or religiousness.

One U.S. study of married couples by Paul Amato and colleagues has found, in addition, that over a period of years when the volume of interactions within marriage were in decline, marital (dis)satisfaction, as indicated by direct reports or thoughts and actions relating to divorce, remained relatively constant: clearly expectations about activities and their contribution to wellbeing can change significantly even over the medium term. They also found that marriages where partners are closer to each other with respect to age, race, religion, and sexual preferences are associated with higher levels of marital satisfaction and lower rates of divorce. And there is evidence of associations between marital satisfaction and rising family incomes, increased husband's share of housework, and the decline of traditional gender attitudes. So while money matters, in a positive way as many would argue, so do a range of other factors that are not obviously or directly related.

In a number of countries increasing numbers of marital unions result in divorce which, evidence suggests, has a significant negative impact on life satisfaction in the first year with substantial recovery that takes places over three to four years. The most frequently cited triggers of divorce include communication problems, basic unhappiness, incompatibility, emotional abuse, financial problems, and sexual problems. Moreover, being in a low-quality marriage is detrimental to various psychological aspects of life quality, particularly support from partner, meaningfulness of role, self-esteem, and stress.

Some of these findings may just reflect the swings and roundabouts of life: two-thirds of those who were unhappy with their marriage at one point report being happy with it five years later. That said, for some in the least happy marriages, things may not improve. Those unhappily married have higher stress levels than others. Overall those who divorce and remain unmarried have greater levels of life satisfaction, self-esteem, and overall health compared with those who are unhappily married.

The question of causality has been raised here as it has in other areas of wellbeing research: does getting married bring about happiness or do happy people choose to marry? Inevitably there are likely to be impacts in both directions but in this case work by Zimmerman and Easterlin suggests that the predominant relation is from being in the states of marriage and divorce to the way we feel while personality appears to play a significant role also. Husband extroversion, for example, has been shown to be a positive factor for both partners' experiences, while own and partner neuroticism is also associated, negatively, with the happiness of both partners.

Children make significant contributions to various aspects of parental life quality, though some studies find a small negative relationship to life satisfaction. To the extent that having children is a matter of personal choice, this finding is something of a surprise. Some evidence points to a reduction in interactions between partners and dissatisfaction with income and these perhaps go some way to explaining the puzzle. However, when people are asked about experience using questions about fulfilment and stress, having children is positively associated with the former and negatively associated with the latter. So different aspects of experience may move in opposite directions for some important life choices and activities and having a more refined approach to understanding our experiences can help to explain some otherwise unexpected findings.

Fulfilment aside, there is some evidence that children contribute to life quality through their impact on the social networks over the life course. Those without children have been shown to have, on average, fewer neighbours and confidants in their social networks, though higher levels of social interaction outside their own household. Marriage (and presumably other permanent relations) also impacts social networks in later life. Both unmarried men and women are more isolated from neighbours and friends than those who are married, but those who have never married have more social ties with friends. A related gender difference derives from the observation that divorced and never married men have been found to be more isolated from family than men who were widowed; finally, it is worth noting that there is significantly less difference in family contact when comparing women in different marital states. Cohabitation prior to marriage is now widespread in many countries around the world and the models of this activity tend to emphasize its role in helping people search for a suitable partner.

Though it tends to take different forms and leads to different consequences for women and men, the issue of domestic violence constitutes a significant challenge to life quality. Data from the U.K. contains some detailed evidence that we have modelled with the following results. The problem can have a significant impact on the overall life satisfaction of those who are at the receiving end, which is hardly surprising in itself, but this helps to make the point that we do *not* always adapt to adverse circumstances as some have seemed to suggest. Furthermore, and perhaps less obviously, there is evidence that fear of future violence has a stronger negative impact on happiness than previous experiences of violence, which suggests that beyond physical acts the expectations and fears of potential victims need to be taken just as seriously. Third, and by applying a method developed initially to quantify the costs of environmental pollution, it has been estimated that the emotional cost of domestic violence could be equivalent to something in the region of 10 per cent of national income. In short, if we are concerned about wellbeing, issues aside from consumption, though possibly related to it, can be rather significant contributors to human wellbeing.

All told, the research discussed in this section suggests, if nothing else, that the wellbeing and happiness we derive from family life is far from simple and not always rosy. Nonetheless, many are drawn to coupledom and family life and the good news is that for a significant number of people, things go well for a large proportion of the time. Research has focused on difficulties related to physical and mental health but valuable lessons could also be learned if we knew more in detail about effective couples and families—how, for example, they negotiate the activities and experiences of daily life and how they develop opportunities for themselves and their children over time. Given that we do seem to know quite a bit about the difficulties, it is perhaps surprising that people do not make greater efforts to search out this information and act on it. Possibly we are the victims of optimistic bias in this regard—the vast majority of drivers claim to be better than average when asked and so perhaps it is with these important social aspects of our lives: we set out with such optimism that we somehow feel we can uniquely overcome the odds, even when they are not in our favour.

Social and Physical Environments

There appears to be less variation in evaluations of social and physical environments, compared with home-related life quality, in part because there are limits to the extent that environments can be personalized. Environments are accessed by all on an equal footing and one problem is that individuals often have little incentive to invest in them.

In general, the evidence suggests that people like where they live with the exception that they are noticeably less satisfied in economically deprived communities. So in this regard, income and happiness would indeed seem to be closely related. Yet the kinds of communities that have evolved vary dramatically around the world. In the U.S., for example, most who could afford a house and a car for decades sought the joys of living in homes with gardens set in suburban areas. In many parts of the world, by contrast, the process of urbanization is still proceeding apace as people migrate from rural areas with insufficient employment opportunities to the apartments and shanties of fast growing cities.

Most people want to live in a safe area and social connections with neighbours might seem to be an obvious aid in this regard; but some studies find that higher levels of neighbourhood ties are not always associated with lower crime statistics. Furthermore, communities which are homogenous, with respect to colour or income for example, tend to be preferred. It is understandable that people who share common interests and goals with their neighbours will get on better but it poses a challenge for policies that seek to support tolerance and diversity. Many countries in Europe are now committed to policies that promote the free movement of labour but have few if any policies that engage with the challenges of social integration that result.

Other things being equal, we tend to be more satisfied with a community the more connections we have with it—whether these be through friendships, work, volunteering, or even just knowing others by name. Taking part in activities for the community is associated with wellbeing at both community and individual levels. People involved in community activity, and with more friends, have higher levels of mental health. Volunteering can foster a sense of cohesion that in turn reduces perceptions of crime and, depending on the type of community involvement, actual crime rates can decrease also. Contributing to after-school activities, for example, impacts positively on education and is associated with lower crime levels. Income, education, and age tend to be positively related to community satisfaction whereas minority group status is often negatively related. It is difficult to be exact about the causality in all of this as involvements with communities grow over time but it is clear that environments have some impacts on life quality and that the rise of online environments is likely to complicate substantially the ways in which social environments contribute to life quality.

From a physical perspective, approximately half of the world's population currently live in cities and the figure is set to rise dramatically over the coming decades. Inevitably this has implications for human wellbeing and happiness at many different levels and raises questions as to how these new urban spaces should be designed. In the U.S., for example, there is a debate about whether there should be a move away from a car-oriented, suburban lifestyle to a denser urban town of 'traditional' design with sidewalks and nearby shops. The impetus for this potential about-turn may have come from environmental concerns to do with car use but one can see a variety of potential and more immediate human benefits. The question is—do people want these benefits? A study led by Kristin Lovejoy, which compared experiences of Californians living in both settings, found that those in traditional urban settings were, in fact, slightly more satisfied with the characteristics of their neighbourhood. Furthermore it wasn't that people valued the key predictors of neighbourhood satisfaction differently—attractiveness and perceived safety were top in both kinds of areas. Nor did suburbanites derive more neighbourhood satisfaction from the quintessential features of suburban living such as school quality, the availability of parking, quiet large yards, or even the presence of cul-de-sacs. Rather, their findings suggested that the urban dwellers derived satisfaction from factors that included liveliness, having close neighbours, and diversity, while the suburbanites were more interesting in living with others of a similar economic status to themselves. The preferences observed probably reflect a mixture of self-selection and adaptation but if, as the researchers point out, urban environments could be made attractive and feel safe, then perhaps they would be more widely appealing.

One method of understanding the values placed on aspects of the physical environment involves looking at the impact on house prices—as a study by two Hong Kong-based economic geographers illustrates. Rapid rises in income across China have reignited the long moribund interest in urban landscapes, though there is often still little by way of official guidelines on the conservation or minimum provision of green spaces. Such spaces, along with water views, are considered attractive and prestigious but without any data on value, it is difficult for builders to know how much, if any, to provide. However, one particularly detailed study found, based on a model of over 600 apartments in Guangzhou, that while having a high ceiling contributes just over 9 per cent to the price of an apartment, being close to a green space or to water adds roughly 7 per cent and 13 per cent, respectively, to the value of a dwelling. Access to green space, particularly, has a range of documented benefits from providing for children's play through to helping people recover from illness, and it is interesting to see how much it can add to the value of a property compared with other features—though such benefits rarely show up in the traditional calculations made by economic planners focusing on housing supply and demand.

Access to Services

Recent equality legislation, for example in the U.K., proscribes discrimination with respect to age, religion and beliefs, sexual orientation, disability, gender, race, and transgender—the so-called protected characteristics. Access to services such as health care and housing are given particular mention but all businesses are required to avoid discrimination, harassment, and victimization on the basis of these characteristics in telephone access and call centres, websites and internet services, written materials, advertising and marketing, the building where services are provided, and the behaviour of staff. This list suggests a wide-ranging contribution that services can make to human wellbeing in modern societies and that most people at some point in their lives will benefit from clarification of their entitlements. (It nonetheless remains something of an anomaly that if an employer or seller is demonstrably discriminating against you on some other non-protected grounds, this is acceptable, legally.)

There is little evidence in our data that people give any consideration to quality of service access when asked questions about overall experience with life and yet denial of access can have significant implications for a person's ability to function normally in society. One standard economic model shows that with appropriate political incentives, governments provide an optimal level of service but the fact is that in many countries, politicians face incentives that are less than ideal. In the first instance, it is difficult for voters to know exactly how much credit to attach to any particular politician and so the incentives for politicians to act appropriately are weaker, in practice, than they should be. Secondly, people have different priorities over services that can cancel each other out—so effective political competition might not help that much. Last but not least, people often vote for political actors sharing their ethnic background and in many situations this can reduce effective competition between politicians who can then become more responsive to their own supporters and less so to other groups.

An interesting example can be found in the comparison of health achievements in Uttar Pradesh and Kerala. These two Indian states had very similar per capita income and poverty rates but quite different levels of human development. While Kerala benefited from high levels of literacy and infant survival comparable to some higher income countries, Uttar Pradesh's outcomes in these areas were similar to some of the poorest countries in the world.

A simple but significant difference was the level of political competition in each State. In the early years of Indian democracy during the middle of the last century, Uttar Pradesh was dominated by the Congress Party whereas in Kerala, the Communist Party provided vigorous and effective competition, in part based on an ability to mobilize large proportions of the population (essentially the poor). The Congress Party faced significant competition in Kerala, which devoted nearly half its government expenditure to education and health services and saw outcomes in both areas rise rapidly as a result.

This connection between effective political competition and the provision of quality services is important as other examples illustrate. In an analysis of public services following the first universal suffrage elections in South Africa in 1994, it was found that perceptions of service quality change (education, electricity, health, road, transport, and water) were significantly related to changes in happiness among rural and urban blacks and was particularly strong among those on lower incomes who might have been expected to benefit most from any improvements. Those who felt happier reported that their residential areas were better serviced than before; similarly, those who observed a number of improvements were more likely to report being happier than those who observed only a few or no improvements.

Health

Health plays a particular kind of role in human development and in this final section we consider it not only in its own right but also as an enabler of opportunity across all the other areas of life. Our framework has emphasized the individual and vastly different talents that people have, the importance of autonomy and freedom, and the value of distributive fairness, and all of these issues are important for health and health services, as we shall see.

Until recently, psychological and psychiatric issues have been something of a Cinderella in the health field, perhaps because it has been difficult to identify effective interventions, or because they fall outside the traditionally historical physical focus of health-care systems. Mental health issues can, nonetheless, be found across the life course emerging particularly in adolescence and early adulthood. Substance disorders have been found, for example by Wittechen and colleagues, to be anything but rare, with abuse being more common than dependency. They found that depressive disorders had been experienced at some point by 16 per cent of a sample aged 14 to 24 whereas the figure for depressive disorders was 14 per cent and for eating disorders 3 per cent. It is not uncommon for those affected to experience more than one disorder and in general they generate significant costs in terms of lost productivity as well as the need for medical advice and treatment. Phobias and impulse control disorders tend to emerge early on in the life course and some three-quarters of onsets have occurred by the time a person has reached their mid-twenties. More severe conditions often follow milder attacks and mental disorders are common also in old age where dementia and depression are particularly prevalent.

Reviews of evidence on effectiveness suggest that interventions aimed at more severe mental health problems can have a beneficial impact, particularly where the design of treatment services is sensitive to the patient's situation. Over time, the difficulty of evidencing successful treatments of some conditions has generated interest in the development of generic therapies aimed at preventing emotional and behavioural dysfunction, but significant gaps in knowledge and implementation persist.

Social skills deficits have been found to be strongly associated with attention deficit, depression, and learning disabilities, particularly in childhood where social problems often first surface. Skills training programmes have been provided as a result but evidence of effectiveness is mixed and not strongly conclusive. That said, there are a variety of approaches that can be used to address these conditions including patient education, self-management, monitoring of depression symptoms and completion of treatment, and technical support for the assessment of medication needs and there is evidence that interventions which combine some of these elements can be relatively effective.

For those at the other end of the age spectrum, early findings concerning depression suggested that *psycho-social* interventions were least effective when compared with chemical or electric-based treatments but there is now evidence that they can have some impact. In addition, exercise in some studies has been positively connected with mental health (particularly compared with sedentary behaviour) which has given rise to the prescription of exercise being proposed as a mental health intervention.

There are, in short, a variety of ways in which mental health can be compromised and these can all have an impact on our capacity to act independently and autonomously. Indeed, autonomy is important for general wellbeing in a number of ways. In the sense of being able to act independently, it has an important role to play in determining what a person's health needs are and how they might best and most effectively be met. Autonomy in practice has social aspects to do with the availability of possible options and societal values, as well as the needs of the individual. It is linked to self-expression, which varies dramatically between people. Facilitating independent living for a person with mental or physical disabilities, enabling people to live happy lives, and providing suitable opportunities for people with rare gifts and talents all require very different activities and policies.

As something we experience, autonomy has a character that changes significantly as our activities and opportunities to enjoy certain kinds of experience evolve over the life course. For children, the development of autonomy is more about getting a reasonable balance of structure and connectedness to carers in daily life. In adolescents, greater autonomy has also been associated with reduced levels of early initiation of sexual intercourse, while those less emotionally attached to their families have been found more likely to engage in behaviours that increase risks to their own health, such as fighting or drug use.

Some thought has been given to how the concept of autonomy might impact on, and ideally be leveraged to enhance, treatment effectiveness. Particularly with respect to long-term conditions, there may be opportunities and incentives for patients to learn how to manage their own treatment. There is some evidence from controlled trials that self-management education which teaches problem solving, in addition to the provision of medical information, improves clinical outcomes in patients.

There is also some evidence that these kinds of problem-solving skills have been useful in reducing costs for arthritis and adult asthma, and that bringing together patients with a range of chronic conditions for problem-solving training can improve outcomes in general practice. One New York-based clinical trial, for example, compared community support for cessation of smoking with an approach that focused on developing a patient-led pathway for quitting. The community approach involved the provision of information and advice to register with a programme or consult their general practitioner. However, in the patient-led approach, patients were asked if they were ready to give up and asked to return in a month or two if they were not. Those who were ready to quit were then invited to nominate a date in the following thirty days to meet with counsellors trained to help and support patients make clear and autonomous decisions. This involved summarizing and acknowledging patients reactions to the information provided. Patients under this more intensive approach were more likely to quit smoking, internalized to a greater degree the motivation to do so, and were more knowledgeable about the mechanisms by which they could limit the negative impact of withdrawal. In short, autonomy can be leveraged to help people benefit effectively from medical interventions and provides a reason for emphasizing mental health—the absence of which can undermine our ability to act independently.

This study from New York illustrates how a person's own choice-making and freedom can be used productively to enhance their wellbeing in situations where, in some sense, they seem to be unfree. The example shows how a simple but carefully thought-through intervention can work in health but it suggests an approach that might be of use in other areas of life that affect our wellbeing. The emerging insights would not quickly be revealed by focusing on income alone (for example paying people to quit or taxing them for continuing to smoke) and in Chapter 4 I want to consider life quality at the ends of the age spectrum where there may be even more to be learned by looking at the direct measures of activity, opportunity, and experience.

QUALITY OF LIFE IN CHILDHOOD AND OLDER AGE

You might spend anywhere between a third and a half of your life not mainly in the work force and this is just one good reason for not assuming that income will tell us everything about your wellbeing. For children and young adults in education, the development of skills and the acquisition of a range of emotional and cognitive experiences are key outcomes and household income is but one input. A parent of average means might create the structure and affection a child needs in its life while one who is wealthy but busy might struggle to deliver these things. Conversely, at the other end of the age spectrum, for those living on relatively fixed pensions, a major challenge may be to find a set of activities that generates a good quality of life through ways that are not necessarily resource-intensive (friendships, hobbies, part-time work, volunteering, and so on). The human flourishing framework introduced in Chapter 2 has been applied extensively to adults but here I want to illustrate how the framework can be used to engage with quality of life issues for younger and older people too.

Early Child Development

Childhood is, *inter alia*, about the acquisition of skills, the exploration of human potential, and the maturation of a personal identity. These outcomes involve activities and experiences that help shape a person's prospects and depend crucially on the opportunities that parents and educational systems provide as a child grows. So long as these outcomes can be measured, the standard techniques for understanding how inputs relate to outputs can be empirically applied. What, we can ask, are good family practices and learning environments for bringing children up? How are these to be tailored by guardians to suit the needs and potentials of different children? What are the key parenting practices in use, how are these distributed across societies and what if anything can we learn from these variations?

We might start by thinking of parental inputs into child development just as we would inputs used by a business to create the outputs valued by customers. Household affluence is important but so too is the parenting regime, especially for very young children not involved in pre-school activity. So too, for that matter, is the quality of the environment outside the household that includes everything from places to play through to facilities for health care. Traditionally, economists emphasized land, labour, and capital as inputs of production and household affluence, parenting regime, and environment can be useful counterparts when we think about the production of life quality at the earliest stages of life. On the output side, we might focus on what children are able to do but also be interested in the activities they are involved in as well as their levels of happiness. These elements are the same as those in adult life but their relevant importance and connections take on a different complexion.

To illustrate how this might work in practice, we estimate models using data from the German household survey and find evidence for a number of points. First, the frequency of activity involvement with a guardian is related to the level of a child's skills. This is after controlling for a number of factors including the child's age, so potentially supportive of the view that parenting interactions are productive. Furthermore, different involvements in different activities are associated with different types of skills. For example, singing by a parent (usually the mother in this sample) is positively related to a child's speech development, controlling for the child's age and a range of other factors. Likewise, involvement in arts and crafts activities is related to the development of motor skills, and visiting other families is related to social skills. To some extent these findings confirm, outside of the laboratory, things that educational psychologists have known for some time, for example, about the development of reading. However, these results can also be taken as emphasizing not just that the home is an important learning environment but rather that if we are concerned about the development of particular kinds of skills then there are likely to be particular sets of activities on which we need to focus.

Findings such as these have, potentially, consequences for policy-making. If the evidence is such that the transmission of advantage between generations starts very early on, so policies to promote social mobility may need to consider ways in which parenting practices in some of the most vulnerable families can be supported if they are to be effective. Furthermore, helping the deprived just by focusing on policies concerning the alleviation of financial poverty may not have much impact on the activities that determine a person's life quality in early childhood.

Parenting, Schooling, and Long-term Benefits

There is growing interest among economists in understanding such issues and particular attention has been given to the evaluation of programmes designed to help children from disadvantaged backgrounds. Delivering significant benefit for relatively low cost is important if there is to be widespread uptake and an interesting example can be found in a state-wide, pre-kindergarten programme launched in Texas several decades ago. Designed to support the academic performance of children deemed at risk (indicated by factors including limited English language, being homeless, and having parents on active military duty) the programme was latterly shown to have generated some useful results and scaled up as a consequence.

Participation in the programme, which was open to 3 and 4 year olds, is associated with higher maths and reading scores and lower chances of not progressing between grades each year or having to receive special services. These impacts have been achieved by a programme that was not lavishly funded, as the evaluators emphasize, and since then there has been an almost universal acceptance around the world in the value of pre-school education starting at around three years of age.

We have already noted that there are important skills not very closely related to academic achievement but conducive to wellbeing and happiness, and such skills are increasingly coming into mainstream focus as work by Nobel Laureate James Heckman and his teams illustrates. Inspired by the human flourishing framework, Heckman argues that overemphasizing cognitive skills misses a raft of things such as 'personality traits, goals, motivations and preferences' that also matter in determining what a person is able to achieve. Personality traits are also, in some sense, skills and therefore amenable to improvement through training and education. The claim may seem a little surprising if one thinks that personality is something relatively fixed but his analysis of the American Perry pre-school programme provides support for the argument. Initially, the programme was designed to enrich the lives of 3- and 4-year-old black children with IQs lower than 85 from low-income backgrounds. Participants were taught social skills through a 'plan-do-review' sequence involving teachers and other pupils—and additional support for parent–child interaction was provided through visits to the home. The programme was scientifically evaluated and initially it was found that there was no improvement in IQ for Perry programme children in follow-up at age 10 compared with a control group. The finding has been used to criticize such programmes but Heckman has found that labour market outcomes some two decades after the programme were improved, *even if IQ at 10 was not.*

Heckman's account for this result is that it was the personality traits, as opposed to the IQ, that were enhanced by the programme. When we look at evaluations other than IQ scores as he notes, student behaviour recorded by teachers covering absences and truancies, lying and cheating, stealing and the use of obscene words was indeed reduced in programme participants. Likewise, measures related to agreeableness and conscientiousness increased. Another U.S. programme, the Use of the Promoting Alternative Thinking Strategies, shows similar results. Its curriculum is used with elementary school children to teach self-control, emotional awareness, and social problem solving and has been shown, through teacher and peer ratings, to reduce aggression, elicit improved pro-social behaviour and enhance academic engagement. Based on the labour market outcome improvements alone, (and therefore ignoring external benefits such as reductions in crime or dependency on state support) it has been calculated that the rates of return to the programme are in the 6 to 10 per cent per year bracket, higher as Heckman delights in pointing out, than those achieved by stock markets over the same period.

In lower-income countries, the themes are remarkably similar even if the relative importance of problems varies with context. Patrice Engle and colleagues estimate, for example, that some 200 million children in emerging market economies do not reach their full developmental potential. Recognizing this shortfall—and no doubt with more than an eye to the financial implications for governments, over thirty countries have initiated programmes to improve child development which, by the mid-2000s, had received some $1.6bn worth of loan finance through the World Bank.

Typically these programmes sought to improve individual parent–child interactions or take a more comprehensive approach using a variety of media to disseminate information to mothers after birth. Engle and her colleagues conducted a meta-analysis of some twenty of these evaluations that had data on both medical issues as well as cognitive and social functioning and on this basis found relatively strong evidence that failure to develop human potential in pre-school children is driven particularly by iodine and iron deficiencies as well as *inadequate cognitive and social-emotional stimulation*. The rates of return to pre-school programmes designed to address these gaps have been estimated as being very high.

Despite potentially impressive rates of return, levels of pre-school investment are relatively low in the developing world with only just over a third of children being enrolled in such programmes at the turn of the century. Engle and her colleagues point to governmental responsibilities and suggest that the absence of a single responsible government department is partly to blame. Is child development a health issue, an educational issue, or an issue for parents? And if the latter, how can parents be reached and supported in countries where the levels of illiteracy among mothers themselves can be over 50 per cent. Furthermore, the whole issue of lost potential is not easy to make visible as it concerns possible benefits in the distant future foregone, rather than actual benefits lost in the here and now: and even for a government with an eye on future benefits, there is a significant question about where the upfront funding costs are going to come from.

All these results about learning mechanisms and the intergenerational transmission of skills raise questions about the design of parenting programmes and there is some research which helps to confirm what we might already suspect. Ineffective parenting behaviours, including inconsistent discipline, nagging, and vague commands, have been identified as contributors to the emergence and persistence of conduct disorder. Effective interventions to reduce these behaviours have been found to require that both the relationship and the behaviours need to be addressed. Typically, programmes designed to reduce these problems have focused on the effective use of praise, descriptive commenting, encouragement, physical positive behaviours and affect, and structured play sessions involving parent and child.

Life Quality in Adolescence

Research on life quality in older children has tended to focus on positive indicators in physical, cognitive, social, and economic areas of life as well as markers of deficits in these areas. Some social scientists have emphasized the mental, physical, and social dimensions and a family's ability to support needs in these areas, while others have argued for an 'ability to successfully, resiliently and innovatively participate in the routines and activities deemed significant by a cultural community'. There has also been an emphasis on internal states of mind, particularly concerning life circumstances and personal problems, in some cases involving a group of closely connected concepts around self-esteem, purpose, and confidence. Complementary studies in economics have looked at the development and transmission of opportunity either through education or social mobility and taken together, many aspects of life quality in adolescence have been researched.

One particularly interesting piece of work derives from a study of over 36,000 adolescents in Minnesota covering social and psychological issues with a particular focus on the factors that protect teenagers from the risks of falling into poor mental health. In behavioural terms, the study highlights two clusters of problems—what it calls 'acting out' behaviours from multiple drug use through to practices that elevate the risk of pregnancy—and 'quietly disturbed' behaviours that run from eating disorders through to suicide attempts. Boys have been found more prone to the former, and girls the latter, though the division is by no means exact.

There are, in addition, some sex differences in the factors that help reduce the probability of these behaviours, though generally, *connectedness to family and school* are the most prominent. Both are statistically more significant than other factors including being in a two-parent family or a family not experiencing poverty, domestic violence or parental substance abuse. Being connected to a caring competent adult in a loving, nurturing relationship appears to be a key contributor to adolescent resilience with respect to a range of risks to quality of life. One could speculate, therefore, that a central reason to value good work–life balance can be found in the positive social externalities that younger family members might enjoy as a result.

Some studies have found that school-aged children are happier when in the company of peers from families of similar wealth levels.

This appears to be another example of what sociologists refer to as homophily—a liking for similar others and again potentially poses challenges for attempts to promote social integration. Furthermore, there is evidence that stressful life events and personality both have significant impacts on externalizing and internalizing behaviours. The experience of immigrants complements this picture, and in the U.S. shows, for example, that first-generation adolescents experience less depression and more positive wellbeing compared with native peers. While immigrant youth are at risk of being materially deprived, it has been argued they also benefit from a range of protective social factors including greater parental supervision, low parent–child conflict, and community connections through religion. Most of these differences appear to have disappeared by the second generation but they serve to reinforce the point that social relations and life quality in adolescence are closely connected.

Evidence from a number of studies suggests that programmes which enhance personal and social skills of adolescents and other children can demonstrate significant improvements in self-perception, school connectedness, positive social behaviours, academic achievement, and reductions in problem behaviours: somewhat related findings emerge from the evaluation of child sponsorship programmes in lower income countries. In such programmes, individuals from richer countries often make regular donations to cover the costs of school uniforms, books and, in many cases, several hours of after-school programmes emphasizing, physical, spiritual, and socio-emotional development. It has been argued that low aspirations can lead to poverty traps and there is some supporting evidence that these after-school programmes contribute to improved attainment by helping to raise the expectations of enrolled pupils. How ever they achieve their impact (selecting of better students is not always easy to rule out), such programmes have been shown to improve the probability of salaried employment by some 5 per cent to 6 per cent. In short, it seems important to enable young people to connect with parents and form social relations with others. The evidence suggests there are immediate behavioural and experiential benefits but also potentially advantages in terms of pathways to key outcomes in adult life, such as employment. At least some of the mechanisms and issues by which human wellbeing is promoted in childhood seem to fit well our human flourishing framework though there are inevitably some significant departures in detailed findings for adults. The question we now consider is what the framework can help us say about life quality in older age.

Wellbeing over 50

The Beatle's song which asks 'will you still need me, will you still feed me, when I'm sixty four?' highlights some timeless concerns that people have as they approach middle age and beyond. Life expectancies continue to rise in most countries, significantly by historical standards, and as a result our social, physical, and material needs pose an evolving set of challenges as we get older. At the age of 50, many might now expect to live another thirty to forty years, the majority of that time in reasonable health, so it is important to understand the factors that contribute to life quality in this phase of life. If in senior years, opportunities to earn an income become more constrained, it is arguably all the more important that we understand how to generate as much wellbeing from a relatively fixed set of resources to which we have access. Of course, it may also be that extending opportunities to do part-time work, or volunteering is an important way forward.

In any case, an interesting window into life quality during the period 50 to 90 is provided by the English Longitudinal Survey of Aging (ELSA) that records some of the most frequently reported leisure activities (eating out, reading a newspaper, and pursuing a hobby, etc.). Differences between the sexes, though they are not so large as to confirm the view that men and women originate from different planets, do indicate that at the margin, older women go outside their homes less than older men (controlling for financial status) despite obtaining pleasure from such activities. For women, models of life satisfaction controlling for wealth and other factors indicate that eating out and being a member of a social club are positively associated with life satisfaction whereas internet use, the one area where men and women do seem to differ qualitatively, is negatively associated.

For men, there is some rather weak evidence that being a grandparent is negatively related to overall experience. One common theme here is that internet use by older women and being a grandparent for men are indicative of being constrained in some way. Perhaps for women, increased internet use is associated with not being able to have face-to-face contact with family and friends. Likewise, and particularly for men, being a grandparent is an external event which may bring with it duties that are challenging or stressful. As we saw earlier, these might have a positive impact on fulfilment measures of experience even if they have a negative impact on satisfaction measures.

For older men, going to the cinema, a day trip in the last 12 months, and being married are all positive factors in models of life satisfaction. The positive effect of marriage for men has been well known for a long time but it is interesting to see that the effect carries over into this age group. The data can be used to ask about the factors that allow these activities to be produced, and it is worth noting that income is never statistically significant whereas age, gender, and educational status often are, and that health sometimes is. Material deprivation in old age is a serious threat to wellbeing but these results also indicate that activity involvement, even controlling for financial status, has an important and not always obvious impact on experience.

An interesting feature of the ELSA is that it asks people not only about the frequency of activities but also about whether they would like to do them more often. This allows us to investigate how frustrated, or otherwise, particular groups are and in what activities they are most constrained. The models show that even controlling for usual suspects (wealth, age, education, marital status, and health) women are significantly more likely to want to participate in all the activities for which data exist. As the relevant activities asked for are all done outside the home, it may be that there are social norms, for example, about eating out alone, that make them less likely to do these things even though their preferences are rather similar to those of their male counterparts.

Some gerontologists have expressed concern that research, and practice, is overly focused on a biomedical model of life quality in older age and these findings help to illustrate the fact that inequalities in older age have significant social determinants also.

In effect, biomedical model defines life quality in old age as the absence of disease and the maintenance of physical and mental functioning, and encourages a focus on clinical responses to deficiencies in these areas. Health researchers, like Ann Bowling for example, have argued for a much broader model that contains socio-psychological factors ranging from life satisfaction through to personal growth and invites contributions to issues of definition from older people themselves. Our human flourishing perspective would seem to support this argument.

Older Age

As people move into even older age, the production of wellbeing and happiness can be expected to change. One Danish study that examined the life quality of frail 85 year olds found having close friends and living with others were most important for everyday life satisfaction and that this was more valuable than regular telephone contact with children. In addition, the researchers found that life satisfaction is higher if people can manage without home services and suggested this was evidence of a strong desire for independence and self-determination. The study also found that being occupied as usual, and using a person's own resources, were also associated with higher life satisfaction. In short, there is evidence, even from late on in life that key aspects of human flourishing—in this case autonomy, activity involvement, and the ability to socialize—remain important contributors to a person's quality of life.

Findings such as these can and do feed into the design of policy and practice. In the early 1980s, the Danish parliament, for example, established a Commission on Aging which critiqued previous regimes for viewing aging solely as a process of decline. Instead it argued that attention should be given to the possibilities that older age afforded, for example to the development of social networks for older people and supporting them in their social roles. This is a significant part of what the Danes mean by care in the community. In this situation older people want ongoing social contact but they do not seem to relish the residential care or home care services sometimes used to make this possible. As currently designed, these seem to undermine other important goals to do with personal freedom, the use of our own resources, and even continuity of existence between one phase of life and the next. As we age, we still want to be involved in at least some of the activities that have filled our time and that we enjoy. When such activities are given up, it is worth asking whether this is from choice and because we are ready to let them go, or simply because the care setting is one in which they would be difficult to pursue. What the Danish experience suggests is that focusing on care regimes that help people to support themselves may well add to the quality of life in later old age.

Autonomy at the End of Life

Even at the very end of life, the choices we make can have a significant impact on our wellbeing and so I want to conclude this chapter by considering some of the issues that arise. At this point and perhaps especially at this point in life, the experiences we have are important not only for ourselves but may also affect those around us. In many countries, patient autonomy continues to be given increasing emphasis and has often been associated with a person's right to decline further treatment though, more recently, such interpretations have been questioned as, in practice, preferred decision-making styles range from active involvement to delegation to an expert clinician. Some would rather not discuss various scenarios explicitly with their doctors, preferring instead to take each day as it comes while others indicate that relatives should have the final say in situations where they can't make decisions for themselves. For at least some, what matters, it seems, is the ability to shape care priorities and have psychological and social needs met without necessarily being involved or consulted about every decision.

In one survey of doctors from six European countries, it was found that end-of-life decision-making preceded between a quarter and half of all deaths studied. Such decisions typically consider the withdrawal of treatment, the prescription of painkillers in doses that may well shorten life, and the involvement in acts that assist a patient to end their own life (which may or may not be legal). When patients were competent, such decisions were discussed in between 42 per cent (Italy) and 92 per cent (Netherlands) of cases. When patients were not competent, decisions were discussed with nursing staff, but not with other caregivers, in over 40 per cent of cases (Italy and Sweden). These levels of communication with family-carers may seem low when compared against recent American proposals suggesting that clinicians should assess the desire to be directly involved in decision-making; articulate a commitment to understanding patient preferences; base treatment recommendations on stated patient goals; and discuss a patient's ideal approach to decision-making should they become incapacitated. Where patients are already unable to be involved in decision-making about their treatment, it may be possible to find a close relative who does know what a person might have wanted had they been able to say. These proposals also recommend discussion of factors considered important to the family and their interests particularly as givers of care. Decisions in this case, should, it is suggested, be presented as a responsibility shared between clinician and family and families should be given permission to opt for palliative care instead of aggressive medical intervention focused on prolonging life.

Life quality, we might conclude, seems to be a rather dynamic affair at both ends of the age spectrum and the balance between experience and opportunity that we pursue is constantly evolving. Beyond income, autonomy and social connections seem to be important contributors to life quality at most stages in life even if what they involve or require varies significantly as we age. In any case, having taken briefly this life course perspective, I now want to focus on some of the cross-cutting themes that emerge through economics, psychology, and ethics in Chapters 5, 6, and 7.

CHAPTER 5

THE ECONOMICS OF HAPPINESS AND WELLBEING

Income and Happiness

A significant strand of economics research into quality of life seeks to understand the relationship between income and life satisfaction and thereby to address one of life's ultimate questions—does money make us happy? The simple question does not, always, lead to straightforward answers and in this chapter we shall look at some of the relations between life satisfaction, income, age, employment, and the affluence of others that have featured in this field. A natural starting point for this work can be found in the work of Richard Easterlin who showed that throughout a decade of significant GDP growth, average levels of life satisfaction in the U.S. population had remained relatively flat. One can argue that as income is unbounded, and life satisfaction was reasonably close to the top of the measurement scale at the start of the period, the result was not that surprising but it helps to raise questions about the reasons for pursuing income growth. If asked, most people would say they would be better off if their income were increased and yet—in terms of our experience of life—it seems it doesn't actually push the needle over the long term.

The paradox has been challenged more recently in a survey of the 'new stylized facts' about income and happiness in which three economists have suggested that life satisfaction is, in fact, positively associated with income and that this constitutes a refutation of the Easterlin paradox. Their observations include the facts that: richer people report higher life satisfaction than poorer ones; richer countries have higher per capita experiences than poorer countries; economic growth over time is related to rising life satisfaction; there is no satiation point beyond which the relationship between income and wellbeing diminishes.

This body of evidence serves to make the point that connections between wellbeing outcomes and income inputs can be assessed in a variety of ways, that comparisons at one point in time take a form of their own, and of course that important positive connections between experience and income can be found. However, much if not all of this evidence is also consistent with the fact that experiential measures of life satisfaction are relative judgements. For example, when comparing countries, the relationship between income and life satisfaction flattens off after a country's average income reaches about $15,000 (in 2005 prices)—not a huge sum for average households in high-income countries. More income beyond this will enable you to consume or save more, of course—but don't expect to *feel* much better as a result.

Employment Income and Health

Job design and unemployment can have particularly significant impacts on experience. Using data on thousands of working age adults in Germany, one early study found that the negative impact on life satisfaction of being unemployed was some three times that of being in bad health. There were considerable variations across the life course, however, with younger people being particularly affected; for at least some older people, the decision to not be employed reflects a positive choice to retire so the study leaves open a question about the impact of forced unemployment. Nonetheless the effect on experience when compared with health problems is rather surprising and provides a reason, additional to the obvious financial ones, for making sure that young people have access to decent work.

And indeed, a review by psychologists covering over a hundred empirical studies confirms that unemployed individuals have lower psychological and physical wellbeing and, therefore, provides evidence that, for a large proportion of the young, being without work is not a state freely chosen. The same study finds, in addition, that while the duration of unemployment has an impact on mental health, the level of unemployment benefits does not. Most significantly perhaps, for those who are unemployed, the centrality of work in their lives, their personal, social, and financial resources, time structure and coping strategies are more strongly related to experiential wellbeing than is human capital—at least as measured in terms of educational attainment.

Coping strategies can play an important role by helping people in their search for work and managing their emotional reactions to the lack of decent and full employment. Repeated but unsuccessful job search is inevitably discouraging and dealing with emotional responses could help people through difficult periods. There is evidence, for example, that people restructure daily life in response to spells of unemployment in very different ways: some are able to organize their time, keep a sense of purpose, carry on with their activities, and avoid excessive dwelling on the past while others find all of these things a challenge.

There is also some evidence that worklessness has an impact on future outcomes. Psychological wellbeing and physical wellbeing are not statistically associated with chances of returning to work (according this review), suggesting that either these variables are poorly measured or that environmental factors are much more important predictors of the return to work. In addition, previous spells of unemployment have been shown to reduce life satisfaction, for both those in employment as well as those out of it. In other words, unemployment has the capacity to leave a psychological scar on those who experience it and, given the implications for future prospects, it would seem that the impact is well founded.

In the first half of the twentieth century, governments were concerned about unemployment because of the potential impacts on productivity, destitution, and perhaps results at the ballot box. In many high-income countries today, the existence of welfare states can, for some, limit the risk of certain aspects of destitution such as hunger but the evidence on quality of life impacts suggests that losses of structured activity, both in terms of appropriate cognitive challenge and social inclusion, are substantial and provide real motivation for seeing the provision of suitable and decent work as one of the most important objectives for societies today.

Economists and public health researchers alike have been interested in the relationship between income and health. Considerable attention has been given to the fact that people who are relatively well off have a higher chance of being in good health and this socio-economic gradient of health operates both within and between countries. The difference in life expectancy between the rich and the poor is about a decade in the U.K., for example, while the difference between countries around the world is nearly five decades. If we are concerned about income inequalities then perhaps we should be even more concerned about health inequalities: some people can expect to have nearly two lives compared to others.

Work on social determinants of health inequalities, led by public health expert Sir Michael Marmott at University College London, has highlighted a diverse range of causes including stress, experiences in early childhood, social exclusion, work, unemployment, social support, addiction, nutrition, and transport. These factors apply both to communicable and non-communicable diseases and income is by no means the only or main issue—food and drink being notable examples. Although hunger still exists in parts of the world, obesity and alcohol addiction are also significant and growing sources of poor quality of life. There has also been some interest in the connection between income inequality, power, and health. The basic argument is that where there are substantial income inequalities, powerful groups are able to change rules governing health provision further to their advantage; to date, however, the evidence for this line of thinking is not conclusive.

Relativities

In 1899, Theodore Veblen drew attention to the fact that personal wellbeing depends on social standing. Some consumption, he maintained, was essentially not for the purposes of need or even direct entertainment but rather a form of social display designed to attract those in a similar position and ward off those who were not. We are curious to know how others are doing and use this information to create benchmarks for the assessment of how well we ourselves are doing. So a person's wellbeing is, to some extent, a relative judgement by definition.

A study in 1978 by Philip Brickman and colleagues drew attention to the dynamic consequences of relative judgements by interviewing lottery winners, accident victims, and a control group who were neither winners nor victims but had otherwise similar characteristics. The aim was to show the importance of adaption to change which, it was argued, took place through the processes of contrast and habituation. According to their theory, judgements based on contrasts and significant changes, even beneficial ones, can make other remaining aspects of life appear quite different even if they have not changed, so we have the capacity to adapt and become accustomed to regular events and behaviours. Initially, a person might compare a new situation to an older baseline but with the passage of time, the baseline evolves until a new framing of events becomes the status quo—as the study found. Lottery winners felt good about winning a large sum of money but they were not subsequently happier than non-winners and in fact took less pleasure from their involvement in a range of everyday tasks. The contrast between the win, and the ordinary activities of everyday life, was sufficiently large and salient that it actually impaired the ability to enjoy life. Comparisons also mattered to those who had been accident victims but in a different way. There was no evidence that victims valued involvement in daily activities more highly compared with the control group though they did value more highly their previous activities which they could no longer enjoy. Taken together, these findings help to account for the widespread tendency for people to be averse to risk. If we adapt more completely to gains than to losses, then it is not surprising that we should do more to avoid negative changes in our situation.

Other people can also be a significant source of benchmarks as Erzo Luttmer has shown using data on the happiness judgements of some 10,000 American adults over the period 1987 to 1994. Strikingly, Luttmer finds that an increase in a neighbour's income has a negative impact on a person's own happiness, that the impact is greater for those who socialize more, and that the impact is sufficiently large that an increase of a neighbour's income by 1 per cent is roughly comparable to a fall of 1 per cent in a person's own income. Anyone who has seen the musical *Avenue Q* will recognize the relation to *schadenfreude* which Gary tells Nicky is 'happiness at the misfortune of others' though this seems to be a mirror image phenomenon, namely one in which we become unhappy at the fortune of others. Sociologists using German data find evidence of similar social comparison effects which, though smaller in size and not found between friends and relatives, suggests that the phenomenon is in part a general human tendency.

Economic Inequalities and Social Mobility

Economic inequalities, as measured in terms of incomes for example, are on the rise and of increasing concern around the world. These are generally discussed with the aid of the Gini measure, according to which inequality has risen significantly over the past two centuries. The reasons and theories are complex but experts cite first and foremost technological change, followed by international trade, declining minimum wages, a fall in unionization, and rising immigration.

Why does this matter for wellbeing? Broadly there are concerns about the failure of growth to benefit all and there are indications that inequality impacts negatively on various dimensions of life. In the first instance, greater economic inequality is argued to reduce economic growth. If the rich put back less of their income into the economy because they consume a lower proportion of income, then economies that give high proportions of income to the rich will not grow as fast as those where the poor have a larger share of income. A number of empirical studies of developing countries have found evidence supporting just this view so it would seem that one of the benefits of greater equality within a society could be higher economic growth. Many developing countries are not, currently, generating enough new jobs to keep up with their growing populations so higher rates of economic growth might contribute to the generation of jobs and the increase of employment.

A second line of argument is that inequalities lead to a variety of social bads. Wilkinson and Pickett most recently developed an International Index of Health and Social Problems based on homicides, imprisonment, infant mortality, life expectancy, maths and literacy, mental illness, obesity, social mobility, teenage births, and trust, and reported a rather close relationship for some twenty-three high-income countries between their index of bads and the Gini measure of inequality. Impacts on other aspects of wellbeing or contributors to it have also been documented. There is, for example, a negative relationship between economic inequality and political stability: the more unequal a society is, the more likely it is to witness politically motivated violence and leaders being overthrown by unconstitutional means.

Statistical measures of economic inequality are one thing, and everyday perceptions another, as a study into how people think about attitudes to pay differentials illustrates. On average, when asked to estimate the wages of a skilled worker, people give accurate estimates, but in all countries they underestimate by wide margins how much company chiefs are paid. This underestimate is greatest in the U.S. where respondents guessed something over $200,000 per year whereas the true figure at the time was just over $1.3 million per year. There are, perhaps surprisingly, similar attitudes to redistributing income from those at the highest income levels in the U.S., as there are in other countries, though there seems to be slightly less support for reducing differentials at the lower end of the pay scale. In other words, while there is support for the reduction of inequalities, if there were a more accurate understanding of the level of inequality that persists, it is likely people would be even more in favour of redistributive policies.

Inequalities persist over time and one particularly novel piece of evidence for this derives from a study of English surnames adopted first in England by the upper classes and initially derived from early major landowners following the Norman conquest in 1066 such as Baskerville, Darcy, and Mandeville who were successors of the king's feudal tenants—families such as Berkeley, Pakenham—as well as those who often took their place of origin as a surname, as did notable families from Beveridge, Perton, and Puttenham. By comparing the share of these high-status names in the university records of Oxford and Cambridge with their prevalence over time, it is apparent that over the past 900 years privileged families have been particularly adept at holding onto their advantage. Educational status appears to be more closely related between generations than, for example, is height, and the result is that status differences in surnames can persist for as many as twenty to thirty generations. The study also showed that social mobility increased somewhat after 1800 in England but that increases in the taxation of wealth (and income) in the early twentieth century had little impact on its distribution. The processes of inter-generational transmission, based on forces of family culture, social connections, and genetics, have an almost physical law-like grip on social structure, it would seem.

By contrast, the U.S. is often thought of as epitomizing a land of opportunity where merit is valued above history or connections though over admittedly much shorter time periods and based on recent tax records, the evidence is that there are strong connections between parental income during adolescence and a person's income at age 30. Furthermore, there is considerable variation between regions with some states showing relatively high levels of mobility comparable to those found in Canada or Denmark while those who have grown up in the south-eastern states experience some of the lowest mobility rates experienced in any high-income country around the world. Factors that act as a drag on social mobility include residential segregation by race and income. Income inequality is negatively associated with social mobility whereas the quality of the schooling system, from kindergarten to 12th grade, is positively associated with mobility, as are measures of social networks and community involvement. Finally, it is worth noting that family structure is important also—and not just at the individual household level. Areas with relatively high proportions of single-parent families have lower levels of social mobility and, overall, there is strong evidence that social connections within a region contribute to the transmission of advantage, or its lack, across the generations.

A U-shaped Relation Between Life Satisfaction and Age

A topic that has particularly interested economists working on happiness concerns the pattern of life satisfaction over the life course. The issue first emerged through earlier psychological studies, which indicated that experiential measures were relatively flat but perhaps increased slightly around retirement before tailing off in old age. The absence of a straight decline with age was slightly surprising to some but more recent work reveals an apparently robust picture in which life satisfaction is a u-shaped function of age. Early middle age is the point at which life satisfaction is lowest according to this evidence and there are several explanatory candidates. For one thing, it could be that the years of early adulthood and retirement represent transitions into new freedoms, initially from the constraints of home and then, on retirement, from those of paid work. It could also be that the mixture of ways we spend our time changes over time and simply involves a less rewarding or more stressful combination of activities in middle age. It could even be the case that different generations have different average levels of happiness and it might even be that our reference points change as we move through the life course. (Higher education for example is often associated with slightly lower levels of happiness and rates of university participation have risen dramatically over the past three decades in a number of countries.)

In any case, work by David Blanchflower and Andrew Oswald seems to show that the u-shape pattern of happiness over the life course can be found in many, though not all countries. According to some estimates, the age of lowest happiness (usually measured as life satisfaction) varies considerably between countries from 35 and 44 years in the U.K. and U.S., to 64 and 66 years in Italy and Portugal. Further, there is evidence also that birth cohorts exhibit different patterns of happiness with U.S. data suggesting a decline in average happiness from the 1900s on—though no such pattern emerges from European data. Technology and related aspirations might be relevant but the changes in the U.S. and Europe have been somewhat similar over the period so it is difficult to see how they could explain a difference. By contrast, we know from other research that being better off than you might expect to be, given your educational status, is a source of happiness and it could be that a lot of migrants to the U.S. found themselves in precisely this situation, particularly in the late nineteenth century and less so subsequently. Work by Claudia Senik at the Paris School of Economics finds that migrants to France are indeed initially happier on average than their native counterparts and that their families take about a generation for happiness levels to adapt to those of the national average. Perhaps the post-1900s fall in American happiness represents a similar drop for those families who had arrived in the late 1800s.

Another approach to understanding life cycle happiness is taken by Richard Easterlin who tries to understand it as a net difference between a variety of experience drivers. Using data from the U.S., he shows how there can be a relation between age and happiness that reflects, particularly, the effects of financial situation, family life, health, and work. This analysis shows, for example, that a person's satisfaction with their family life peaks somewhere around the age of

50 and then declines, whereas financial satisfaction is lowest some-where around 35 and recovers significantly thereafter. Job satisfaction peaks in the mid-50s while satisfaction with health declines consist-ently throughout adult life—a fact suggesting that on average object-ive health and satisfaction with it are closely related over the life course. During middle age, however, increases in satisfaction with family life and work more than offset the decline due to health. In the later downward phase, satisfaction with health, family, and work all move downwards though these are also partly offset by increasing satisfaction with the financial situation—at least for some of the time.

Notwithstanding this evidence, there has been some controversy as to whether these patterns exist at all. One of the most recent and statistically sophisticated contributions suggests that, because unhappy people tend to drop out of surveys more than others, the rise in life satisfaction that starts in middle age simply reflects the fact that proportionately more happy people are left in the survey as time goes by. When allowance is made for this possibility, the u-shape turns into something that looks more like a wave. Happiness, in the most sophisticated model, is relatively flat between the age of 18 and 60, rises noticeably thereafter to be followed by a major decline after the age of 75. The results over the initial period of working age are consistent with the prediction people will equalize happiness over the life course—in other words, for much of our lives, we are not short-sighted about our future wellbeing—but that still leaves the need for an explanation of the burst of joy in late middle age.

Perhaps the last word on the life cycle of experience should go to a recent and novel study of similar patterns in other species. Based on a sample of over 500 primates in zoos from five countries, the investi-gators asked keepers to rate animals in terms of positivity of mood, pleasure derived from social interactions, success in goal achievement, and a question about how happy the keeper thought they would be if they were the animal they cared for. Using this last measure, the lowest average levels of happiness were found between 28 and 35 years of age, comparable to humans allowing for our higher life expectancy. One interpretation, not so different to that proposed by Easterlin for humans, is that after 35 animals are increasingly freed from the daily stresses of caring for offspring or competing for social position.

Materialism

The question as to whether income makes people happy often leads to related discussions about religion and materialism and, in this final section, I want to consider some findings from research by Robert Barro and others that look at connections between religion and economic growth. At least by some measures over the past three decades, economic growth has been accompanied in the main by a decline in religiosity in many parts of the world. But if, as some hypothesize, religious beliefs sustain a range of behaviours such as thrift, work ethic, and honesty, which are conducive to productivity, then a decline in these values might be accompanied by falling growth rates. The evidence Barro and colleagues looked at only gives partial support to this view. A belief in hell does seem to be connected to growth but church attendance is negatively related to growth. So perhaps church attendance partly reflects different priorities people have though Barro emphasizes an explanation that sees churches as consumers of resources that act as a drain on a country's resources. We should be cautious before rushing to accept this interpretation, however, as churches often deliver social services at no cost to the recipient: such benefits are not reflected in national income figures though they would be if they were supplied by market providers.

Some of these issues are touched on in very different ways by psychological studies that deal with measures of materialism and experiential aspects of wellbeing. People have been asked, for instance, to compare financial success with other values such as psychological growth, autonomy, self-esteem, family life, friendships, and the desire to contribute to community improvement. One finding that stands out from these studies concerns the fact that higher emphases on financial success are associated with greater probabilities of psychological disorder. Elsewhere, Russell Belk finds that there are clusters of behaviour around wanting to keep, own, and not share possessions which are associated with envying others who have things we desire. One of the themes that links these findings is not that materialism is good or bad but rather that it is something we might at individual or societal level trade off against other human values and priorities. And perhaps placing too high a value on material aspects of life quality can be counterproductive for most of us if it encourages us to emphasize the importance of objects that can easily be compared. Some, including the economist John Kay, have argued that individuals should adopt a more oblique approach to the pursuit of life quality and it may be that the partly self-defeating nature of comparisons helps to explain why non-materialists appear better off according to the experiential measures.

At a societal level, however, there is often a need for us to take a view and act on it, and the need imposes limits on implicitness. So what are the consequences? Potentially for economic thinking they could be quite profound. We have seen that work can be a source of considerable satisfaction while the fear of unemployment is a threat to which we do not readily adapt. But if free global trade combined with rapid technological change is leading to increasing job insecurity around the world, then we have a trade-off to consider. Currently, global trade regulations give most weight to consumption but the economics of wellbeing seems to caution against putting all our eggs in that single basket. Connections between employment and a broad conception of wellbeing can be found, if further proof is needed, in literature that spans Steinbeck's raw account of life in 1930s dustbowl America to the desperate blogs that litter the internet by people who in middle age have lost their job, their home, and any real prospect of ever finding work again. We can take several things from the economics of happiness but creating societies that offer productive activity to all, an idea that goes back to Keynes at least, should surely rate high on the list.

CHAPTER 6

PSYCHOLOGICAL MOTIVATION, INTERACTIONS, AND STRATEGIES

For much of the previous century, economists assumed that people were maximizers of their own self-interest. A reasonable starting point perhaps for some purposes, but this rather dry characterization has little to say about the fact that people often feel they do things for a mixture of motives and that benefits to others might, just sometimes, be part of the equation. In recent years, there have been several attempts to address this gap by seeking to explain the conditions under which people do, in fact, consider others, behaviours that are often now described as *prosocial*.

Some of the notable earlier attempts to explain these social elements include theories by two psychologists, Abraham Maslow and Clayton Alderfer, who proposed that human goals and motives form distinct groupings that we pursue in sequence, rather as we might climb a ladder. At base, there are existence needs to do with safety, security, and physiology which we seek to satisfy first. When these needs are met, we move on to relatedness needs such as belonging, connectedness, and affection. Finally, when both these lower order needs are complete, we seek to fulfil a range of high-level needs concerning personal growth, self-esteem, and the actualization of own identities.

The theory tells a plausible story though empirical testing has found it wanting, particularly with respect to the hierarchical structure of needs and wants. It seems that in high-income countries these different groups are given more equal priority than the theory predicts and in the rest of the world there would be doubts too. Even tribal people living in situations where lower order needs have barely been met seem to pursue rather sophisticated social goals. Neither the hierarchy of needs approach, nor the selfish only theory, gets human wellbeing entirely right and so in this chapter I want to consider some of the evidence that helps extend our understanding of what wellbeing is and how we pursue it.

Prosocial Behaviour

One simple starting point is to ask how we might explain actions where consideration of others is a motive? There are several ways to this but the most obvious examples outside family life include purely altruistic acts such as anonymous donations to charity and the leaving of a tip in a restaurant to which you will not return. Pure altruism explains such acts in terms of the benefit received by others, which seems reasonable until we realize that it excludes the benefit to ourselves from the act of giving. Does how we feel about the act of giving not also play a role?

One implication of the pure altruism explanation is that collective provision by government, for example, can make redundant our own need to give. Government activity can 'crowd out' private provision if it makes redundant our own reasons for giving and there is some evidence to support this view. Based on several studies, it has been estimated that for every additional dollar spent by government, individual contributions are crowded out by between nothing and $0.50. In other words, it seems that people do indeed give for reasons that are additional to the benefits they wish to bestow on others and while such actions are not purely altruistic, they are clearly oriented towards the benefit of others.

A second explanation of giving allows for non-recipient benefits and accepts that givers also benefit. Such benefits could be anything between a 'warm glow' derived from the act of giving to more concrete benefits such as the building of a reputation. This explanation of why we give would seem to be more realistic in several situations and yet there are phenomena that it cannot explain. Donor fatigue, the fact that people may, after a while, tire of repeatedly giving for a particular cause, is a well-known phenomenon but not one that can be explained easily by focusing on the reward a person might derive from such giving: if the act of giving is rewarding in itself, why should it not continue to be so over time?

A third approach to gifts and giving highlights the importance of reciprocity, the idea being that a gift is often embedded in some larger concept of exchange. Giving, according to this view may return a previous favour or anticipate some beneficial act in future and it features widely in studies of tribal people. In some accounts of reciprocity, the expectation of return might not be from any named individual. People do things for others, sometimes, just because they believe others in similar situations would probably do the same for them.

In addition to the evidence from anthropological studies, there are now also many related experiments that shed light on how people contribute to collective endeavours. In group settings, there is often an incentive for individuals to free-ride—that is to reduce their contribution to social effort while hoping that no one else does. Such free-riding can undermine group projects but when there is an opportunity to return favours, or punish refusals to collaborate, levels of individual contribution are much higher and can be sustained into the long term. Indeed, many years ago a tournament between different computer programs found that most successful in a wide range of situations was the simple tit-for-tat strategy that rewarded players who had just contributed and punished those who had chosen a more selfish option. The evidence is that, like this program, humans are also reciprocators, though the effect is much stronger when the consequences imposed by others are negative.

Further support for reciprocity-based explanations of giving can be found in attitudes to income redistribution. People who believe that being in need is due to external circumstances are more likely to support the redistribution of income whereas those who feel the needy are, themselves, responsible for their condition do not. In other words, reciprocity and responsibility are connected, a view supported by Yale economist John Roemer who concludes that societies should use general taxation to compensate people for the deprivations that are not of their own making. Other examples include the finding that taxpayers reduce their claims for government rebates when they learn that the levels of tax compliance are higher than they had imagined. Similarly, it has been found that cross-country skiers are much more willing to contribute to the up keep of tracks when they learn that others are also.

Both giving to others and collective endeavours are, in short, haunted by the serious problems of incentives and free choice, but equally, when an activity is widely desirable, there are several ways in which we can understand why and how people give freely or come close to doing so.

Friendship

True friendship cannot be bought and consumed, we are told, but this vital if sometimes fragile and elusive form of social contact contributes to wellbeing and happiness in a range of ways over the life course. Aristotle proposed that there were three types of friend: those that serve instrumental purposes; those based on the sharing of emotional bonds; and a third category derived from our admiration of a person's virtues. From colleagues at work to confidants and lovers, and perhaps even mentors or figureheads, Aristotle's categories seem as applicable today as they did to him 2500 years ago, suggesting that friendship is a universal contributor to human wellbeing. Human friendship is inextricably bound up in our minds with choice (you can choose your friends but not your family) but before coming onto this I want to explore briefly what might be learned from the now extensive body of research on relations in other species.

From the 1960s on, scientists have examined the affective systems of a growing range of species. Different pairings have measurably different intensities of bonding—for example if non-human infant primates are separated from mothers, their distress can be predicted by the level of active physical engagement with their mothers prior to separation. Indeed, major separations early on in life have been shown to have long-term impacts on behaviour—something previously believed only to occur in humans.

Bonds between pairs in other species can exist over long periods of time and take very different trajectories between the sexes. Young baboons of both sexes interact a lot, not only with mothers but also with siblings, aunts, and grandmothers. However for males, bonds with the mother's family decline until adolescence at which point male offspring migrate to another group. Females, by contrast, stay within the group and a social ranking emerges between them and their families that remains relatively stable over time. And there is considerable variation even within the non-human primates. Chimpanzees, for example, live in communities that form temporary groups of between two and fifty during the day where males are more active socially than females. At maturity, and in contrast with young baboons, it is the female who leaves the group into which they were born while males remain.

A significant aim of social interaction in primates is the fulfilment of current needs: they often engage in mutual grooming, for example, where reciprocity is immediate. In some cases, female primates will groom the mother of a new-born infant in return for permission to touch her infant. Whether such encounters can be planned is not known though it is clear that memories of previously pleasurable activities form a basis on which social interaction takes place. There is evidence, too, that other species recognize the different relations between other members of their social groups. Calls for help or responses to aggression are sensitive, not just to the nature of an attack but also the social ranking of potential allies present and even the social connections of those who might be subject to retaliation.

Across a range of species, there is motivation to form at least one enduring social bond, often with close relatives but sometimes with more distant relatives, particularly age-mates, when demographic factors prevent bonding with a more closely-related partner. Current evidence suggests the capability to form such bonds is related to survival. Female baboons with relatively stable social relations enjoy higher infant survival and live longer. Similarly, female horses and dolphins with stronger social bonds show higher birth rates and levels of infant survival, while for male dolphins and chimpanzees the ability to form alliances and bonds is related to reproductive success.

Findings from other species should not be applied directly to our own experience of course but they provide a useful backdrop against which to understand some of the dynamics of friendship. So what of human friendship? As the educationalist Mary Healy points out, friendships in childhood help us start finding out who we are, what we value, and even who we might wish to become. In adult life, and work especially, we might spend considerable amounts of time with those who share our interests, but are otherwise quite different to us.

Social skills are significantly developed by cognate activities from a very early age. By age six, children are able to discuss the connections, for example, between play and friendship even though such connections may be short-lived. In addition, they can recognize that being a source of happiness is important in friendship and that there are some conditions, such as grief caused by the loss of a pet, that permit exceptions to this rule. Friendship in childhood is a source of learning as well as happiness but for some children, such as those with forms of autism, basic social and conversational skills, such as initiating conversation and turn-taking, are difficult and need to be taught.

Compared with young children, adolescents rate their friendships as more intimate, which could reflect either spending more time with other children or a better understanding of thoughts and feelings. On average, girls, more than boys, share information with friends who they value for listening and understanding and this difference carries over into adult life. Those with more supportive relations have higher self-esteem and are better adjusted to school though it is not easy to say much about causality based on these correlations alone. Attitudinal data on supportive relations for this age group suggests that the benefits of positive friendships are substantial though there are situations where friends can have negative impacts on behaviours, particularly where groups are extremely cohesive and use physical violence to maintain group membership and conformity.

Studies of friendship formation in early adulthood, for example of students going to university for the first time, highlight also the importance of chance, proximity, and race. One experiment found that sitting next to someone, or even in the same row, for long enough to make a short introduction, had an impact on friendship relations a year later. Another study that looked at emails between U.S. university students found that being in the same dorm had a significant impact on interaction, as did belonging to the same race. Family background and common interests were also relevant whereas ability as measured by entrance examination tests was not. These particular findings are rather reminiscent of a comment by Peter Ustinov who once suggested that he did not believe friends were necessarily the people you liked best so much as the people who got there first.

As people move towards marriage and parenthood, interactions with friends tend to decline. There is evidence that contributions of a closest friend to companionship, intimate disclosure, affection, reliable alliance, reassurance, emotional support, and instrumental help reduce as the calls of the family unit take over. In married adult life, there is some evidence that having a couple of best friends makes a significant contribution to experienced wellbeing. Having more than two such friendships, in a study of 600 adult Americans across the age range up to seventy-nine, did not have any additional impact on wellbeing nor was there any evidence that friendships could act as a buffer against low-quality family or spousal relations.

The nature of friendship, at least its contribution to wellbeing and happiness continues to evolve as people live longer and technologies mediate the way we interact. The internet has been criticized for contributing to the rise of a society that causes people to be isolated though the picture is complicated as reported numbers of friends (which includes online friends) are increasing, particularly among heavy internet users, so perhaps quantity is not at risk—even if quality might be.

In older age, the need for and benefits of friendship as a resource for beneficial activities and experience may become more important as we live longer. Isolation is becoming a particular issue for people at this stage in life and it may not be a trivial problem to crack. Over a decade ago, a study was designed to provide and evaluate telephone support to help older women who had indicated a problem with loneliness. The system was based around a telephone partnership with someone of a similar age—ideal for people in this position, one might think. In fact, more than a fifth of women contacted did not participate in the study and nearly half of those who did discontinued discussions with their 'partner' before the end of the intervention, facts that led the researchers and others to view the intervention as a rather limited success.

It would be instructive to know why the trial was not more successful and several explanations have been proposed. Possibly most important of all, it has been noted that there were no shared activities in the intervention, which could have helped to bring partners together. Indeed, by focusing on lack of friendship as the common feature, the study designers may have caused the participants to dwell on something from which they should have been distracted. Secondly, there were substantial differences in responses to the programme and it so could be that, with a bit of redesign, a more effective intervention could be developed. Finally, it has been suggested that focusing on kinship ties might have led to better outcomes. The evidence on friendship arguably points in this direction, though the Danish study of the elderly seems also to be suggesting that at this age, face-to-face contact with a friend is particularly valuable.

Personality

Friendship contributes to experiential and other aspects of wellbeing throughout the life course and personality is often a significant determinant of the friends we have. Though they clearly change significantly at either ends of the age spectrum, personality in adult life is generally regarded as relatively stable. One study suggests that just over half the variation in emotional states can be explained by personality traits while external events and situations account for a quarter of the total variation. Further, personality seems to have a strong genetic component: a study of 1400 twins reared apart, for example, found that happiness was highly correlated for identical twins but that there was almost no relationship for other twins. Extraversion, of all the big five personality traits, is the most closely related to self-reports of happiness and one possible explanation is that extroverts have brains that get more out of positive experiences. This close relationship between genes and experiential measures of happiness has led psychologists to suggest that we all have our own personal natural level of happiness. However, some introverts are also relatively happy, a fact that Michael Argyle shows is consistent with introverts taking part in social activities often pursued by extroverts. So notwithstanding the power of our genetic make-up activities seem to matter also.

Other aspects of personality, including self-control, personal esteem, optimism, and purpose in life, have also been shown to be connected to experiential aspects of happiness. The concept of internal control is a psychological measure of the extent to which a person believes he or she is responsible for the outcomes they experience, as opposed to external forces or fate, and many studies show that high levels of internal control are indeed related to high levels of happiness. It is not difficult to see why this might be the case if those who find they are able to achieve the goals they pursue will tend to be happy as a result, while those who are less successful feel they are buffeted by life and that their actions often have little impact on the outcomes they experience. Similar observations apply to optimism: a positive frame of mind can lead people to expect good things in future, recall good things from the past, have a positive view of others, and judge stimuli to be more pleasant and these positive expectations, particularly of others in social interactions, can to a degree be self-fulfilling. There may also be sustained, significant physical benefits as at least one study has found a connection between levels of optimism and the activity of the immune system several months later.

Finally, and from a motivational perspective, there is evidence that having meaning and purpose in life is also connected with happiness. Cantor and Sanderson, have for example, emphasized the importance of 'participating in valued activities and working towards personal goals', activities thought to offer a sense of agency through challenge, structure, and meaning in daily life. Appropriate activities help with our ability to cope with life's ups and downs and to form social relations: furthermore the effect on experience is greater if activities are freely chosen, goals are realistic and mutually compatible, and substantial amounts of time can be devoted to goal-relevant activities. Cantor and Sanderson's psychologically-oriented proposals fit well the theoretical framework discussed in Chapter 2 and help to highlight how various aspects of wellbeing can feed into and complement each other. The message seems to be that freedom and choice are important (a view that economists emphasize) but need to be married to structured activity and a sense of having some control over our everyday lives (which psychologists emphasize). The former without the latter could be disorientating while the latter on its own could lead to routines that don't suit most of us at all. But personality isn't the only important resource for wellbeing, and sometimes people do seem to get 'locked' into routines that are not at all good for them or those around them, as we shall now see.

Absorption and Burnout

An interesting piece of research relating to intense experiences of purpose, which first emerged in the 1970s and has subsequently been highly influential in psychological circles, concerns what the American psychologist Mihaly Csikszentmihalyi has labelled 'flow'. In its extreme form, flow is a state of mind in which a person is so absorbed in what they were doing that the activity makes them oblivious to everything else. The idea started from the observation that visual artists can persist, single-mindedly ignoring normal daily activities, until a painting is complete and at that point they completely lose interest in what was the work. This state of being has a number of features: intense and focused concentration on current activity, the merging of action and awareness, unawareness of oneself as a social actor, a sense of being in control, a distorted sense of time passing, and experience of the activity as rewarding in itself. Sports and games (chess notably) are said to be particularly conducive to creating this state of being though ultimately it is the fit between skills and tasks, as judged by the actor, that matters. Rewarding as such tasks are, they sit precariously on a cusp between activities that are not sufficiently challenging and lead to boredom and those that are so demanding they produce only discomfort and stress.

There have been many applications of this concept in practical settings. In one U.S. public school, the idea was incorporated into the curriculum by timetabling regular opportunities to actively choose and engage with activities related to students' interests which were then pursued without external demands or pacing. Other applications include the organization of police work, psychotherapy interventions, and product design, as well as the development of certain key skills in children. 'Complex' families, for example, have been found to be ones that simultaneously provide support and challenge. Children from such families spend more time in high-challenge, high-skill environments than children from families where only support or challenge is provided. Children who are both challenged and supported tend to feel more in control of their actions and better in themselves. Moreover, tasks that provide the right level of challenge can be both engaging and facilitate learning. The emphasis on autonomy that comes from this psychological research is one shared with the human flourishing framework and it is important to note that it is possible to use carefully judged freedom in education and family settings to enable people to pursue the goals they value.

By stark contrast, and at the opposite end to flow is a phenomenon known as burnout, which psychologists have defined as a 'syndrome of emotional exhaustion and depersonalization' that generally leads to decreased effectiveness at work. The phenomenon has been explored in numerous studies including one by Johns Hopkins medical school in which researchers analysed quality of life and mental health survey responses from over 7000 surgeons around the U.S. Using a measure of burnout based on over twenty items, the study found that nearly one-third of all surgeons who replied had high scores on emotional exhaustion, that about a quarter indicated high levels of depersonalization, and over 10 per cent indicated a low sense of personal achievement. The researchers estimated that some 10–15 per cent of their respondents could have been diagnosed as having a major psychological disorder, a finding consistent with the fact that clinicians are widely known to have lower than average levels of mental health.

Looking at a variety of potential risk factors for burnout, the researchers found certain family characteristics to be relevant. Being younger and having a spouse employed outside the home as a non-healthcare professional increases risk, while having children reduces it. Job characteristics associated with burnout included: area of speciality (a small number including trauma and general surgery were particularly prone); higher number of nights on call; longer weekly working hours; more years in practice; and having compensation entirely based on billing. By contrast, having more than half of a surgeon's time dedicated to administration, education, and research, that is, non-clinical work, reduces the risk. Nearly 40 per cent of responding surgeons met the criterion for burnout, half said they would not recommend the profession to their children, and only one-third felt that their career gave them enough time for personal and family life.

The study paints a somewhat surprising picture of what must be one of the best remunerated professions on the planet and raises questions as to why, if these threats to the wellbeing of highly paid staff are so widespread, organizations are not taking greater steps to prevent them. Perhaps the difficulties do not substantially affect hospital billing and possibly any increases in early retirement or resignations that might result can be offset by the appointment of younger and less expensive surgeons. In any case, the fact that compensation related entirely to billing is a risk factor for burnout suggests that the incentive structure faced both by the hospital and the individual plays a significant role in the life quality of these employees. But perhaps the most important issue this research raises concerns the extent that we can rely on the economic interests of companies to help us protect and sustain the quality of our lives. Even for employees who are very valuable to an organization, it seems the incentives to support life quality might not always be that powerful.

Wellbeing Games

Hospitals around the world can face incentives that are perverse and lead to poorer outcomes than would otherwise be the case. Generally it is the structure of the social interactions that gives rise to difficulties as the following examples from game theory indicate. Economists have specialized in recent decades in studying how the structure of social interactions can impact on our outcomes and in this section I want to illustrate how some of this analysis can be applied to understanding the wellbeing outcomes that we end up with.

Suppose, for instance, that Ana and Ben want to go out together but would prefer different forms of entertainment. Ana wants to go to a soccer game and Ben wants to visit an art gallery. However, both would prefer to be doing something together rather than something on their own. What will they do? With suitable payoffs, this so-called 'battle of the sexes' game can be shown to lead to two significant outcomes in which Ana and Ben both go to the soccer or they both visit the art gallery. These are equilibrium outcomes in the sense that if either outcome is what they intend to do, then there is no reason for either to change their mind. If they are decided to both go the game, Ben has no reason to visit the gallery, though that is what he rather do if accompanied. Likewise if both were minded to visit the gallery, Ana would have no incentive to go to the game on her own. However, if Ana and Ben have to decide when they leave work where to go, and for some reason can't communicate, it is difficult to predict what they will do. If there were only one equilibrium, they might both settle on that, but there are two so they can't tell just from the logic of the situation where the other will go. Ana might decide to go to the gallery to be with Ben, but Ben might decide to go to the soccer game to be with Ana. So the outcome could be a co-ordination disaster with Ana at the gallery and Ben at the game, and both on their own. In any case, they themselves don't know how each other will behave and if each picks the equilibrium that gives them most pleasure, they end up going to their own most preferred activity but also, in the words of Robert Putnam, they end up 'bowling alone'.

These analyses and outcomes depend on concepts of social inter-action developed by John Nash, the subject of the film A Beautiful Mind. There are a couple of exit routes from these dilemmas and these are potentially useful devices in a range of settings. One curiously has to do with the ability to reduce our freedom by making a binding commitment, as the game of 'chicken' illustrates. In the 1960s, young Californians played a simple game in which they drove towards each other in their automobiles until one person swerved to the side—or both crashed into each other. It was said that the best way to play the game was to don a pair of very dark glasses before getting into the car, to throw out a whiskey bottle as the car picked up speed, and finally, if the opponent was still driving towards you, to throw from the car window a steering wheel. Such actions bind the player to a course of action and force a reasonable opponent to take avoiding action. Indeed, the strategy of making binding commitments is an old one that can be found even in Homer's *Odyssey* where Ulysses lashes himself and his sailors to the masts of their ships to avoid being lured to their deaths by the otherwise irresistible singing of the Sirens.

Autonomy

The desire to be autonomous, free from the external constraints of others, is deeply rooted but raises questions about the nature and quantity of freedom that we deem desirable. We expect to become more autonomous as we grow up but even then there are significant variations in beliefs about how much autonomy is appropriate and at what age. In Summerhill school, for example, founded by A. S. Neil, everyone from the seniormost teachers to the youngest pupil had an equal vote in the regular meetings that governed the school. Children were not required to go to lessons but rather encouraged to attend those classes that interested them—and the regime broadly survives to this day. Many, *though not all*, pupils flourish in this system and often choose arts-oriented careers as a result. Summerhill is a fee-paying school, and its relevance to the free state sector might therefore be seen as limited but it helps remind us of the potential value of involving people in decisions that affect their lives at most ages.

Autonomy can be explored empirically in many different areas and psychologists have looked at it through a range of experiments— some with adults often using seemingly very trivial choices. It was often assumed by economists that more options would always be better but the evidence suggests this is not always so. For example, people have been asked to choose a gift box for a friend in experiments that varied the number of boxes available. They were then also asked to rate both their choice and the experience and on both criteria, people were most satisfied when choosing from ten items and less satisfied when choosing from a smaller or larger number of options. If we have too many options, then factors such as regret and 'cognitive dissonance' (behaviour which seeks to reduce discomfort brought about by inconsistencies) start to creep in and the increasing difficulty of deciding can outweigh the marginal benefits that additional options might bring. Aldi, a cut-price European supermarket chain, exploits this fact by selling many fewer lines than most of its competitors and is said to sell many more items of each line, in part, as a result.

How we value choice seems also to vary significantly across cultures. When choosing between four pens of one colour and a fifth of a different colour—all otherwise identical—European Americans have preferred the unique pen whereas Asians choose a pen from the majority colour. Differences based on class have also been found: when asked to give three words associated with choice, American middle-class students tend to mention freedom and independence, whereas working-class students offer words such as fear, doubt, and difficulty.

While autonomy might be defined as the ability to act independently of external factors, in many cases this would seem too extreme, as reasoned (and reasonable) behaviour is often a matter of taking external forces into account. Indeed, one of the main psychological approaches to autonomy, known as self-determination theory, emphasizes precisely this interplay between an individual's goals and environmental forces and the fact that extrinsic motivators, like money, can drive out the desire to do things for their own sake. The philosopher Joseph Raz has emphasized the value of being the author of one's own life but reality, it seems, calls for a more tailored view that is sensitive to our identities and opportunities.

Physical Activity

Much of the debate about quality of life and wellbeing centres around social, financial, and environmental issues, but I want to briefly mention the issue of physical exercise. For many people, it is natural, after school to fall into a lifestyle where exercise plays little part in life but even at school social norms around physical appearance can inhibit what should be a normal part of everyday life. Evidence of what is needed to help us engage in activities that are better for our health, given the environment we find ourselves in, can be found in many places including one notable case of Sao Paulo, a Brazilian city which built a large network of walking and cycle tracks that four years later resulted in a 50 per cent drop in hospital admissions for hypertension.

Physical exercise, however, is not just about physical health as it improves mood and reduces symptoms of depression: for major depression there is some evidence that aerobic exercise is more effect-ive than drug-based treatment. Exercise can, in addition, prevent the onset of depression and alternative therapies, such as yoga and African dance, can reduce negative feelings and stress. There is also some evidence that physical exercise can reduce the rate of mental decline in old age, improve self-esteem in adults with Downs syndrome, and produces a range of benefits for children in low-income families. Regular activity also serves as a buffer against the negative mental impact of obesity and this benefit can be found even if there is little significant reduction in body weight.

Physical activity is, then, something we have several reasons to value, and the social environment in which we live plays a significant role in how much of it we take. Social networks are important and have been used in walking groups and buddy systems to help motivate and sustain such activity. Exercising with others helps with learning about health and wellbeing, the establishment of norms in favour of activity, the giving and receiving of positive feedback, and the development of social connections. There are dramatic differences in health outcomes for different groups in society and the same is true of healthy behaviours. Those in higher socio-economic groups are more likely to engage in physical exercise and are quicker to reduce riskier behaviours at a faster rate. Conversely, deprived localities are often also ones where there are fewer appropriate or safe spaces to exercise.

Exercise, in short, is important even in our sedentary age and can generate a variety of life quality benefits. The World Bank has estimated that the state of Sao Paulo managed to save some $310m per year in health care costs and there is now an annual discussion of physical exercise by 200,000 teachers and 4.5 million pupils. Those involved in this initiative suggest there is no single formula to follow though it seems that a bit of inspirational political leadership combined with an efficient administration can help people achieve a lot for themselves.

66 Routes to Happiness

One way to develop insight into what makes people happy is, of course, simply to just ask them and in this final section I want to mention an investigation in which California-based psychologist Sonja Lymbominski and her colleagues did just this. Their primary focus was to understand the diverse nature of strategies that people consciously employed in their search for happiness and the results provide a useful insight into what we know, if only by giving us a handle on what happiness means to people.

In the first stage, an initial group of subjects were asked an open-ended question about the strategies they employed and from over a hundred responses, some sixty-six strategies were selected for inclusion in the main survey. (Route 66 was a highway that took hopefuls to the west coast of America in search of work and so was, for many, literally a path they hoped would lead them out of deprivation.) At the second stage respondents were asked about the use of these strategies as well as their level of happiness in experiential terms. Statistical analysis of strategy use revealed some eight groupings: social affiliation, partying, mental control, goal pursuit, passive leisure, active leisure, religion, and direct attempts to modify mood.

Perhaps the first thing to note about these different strategies is the fact that a number are essentially social or have a significant social aspect to them. Partying comes high on the list and this almost certainly reflects the fact that the respondents were college students but the fact that social affiliation is the most important cluster is something we might expect to find in most groups. Secondly, and while the list of strategies contains a significant share of hedonistic activities, it also contains within it the pursuit of major life goals which in turn comprise the pursuit of career goals, attempts to reach full potential, striving to accomplish things, study and trying to do well, and organizing life and goals. The inclusion of these items is important because the study specifically avoided trying to predefine what activities might be deemed to be part of the pursuit of happiness and instead took its list from what respondents themselves suggested without further prompting. Many of these activities just highlighted will serve to boost the opportunities that people have in particular domains of life, albeit at the cost of opportunities in other areas, so there is evidence that at least some people do define their own happiness sufficiently widely to include the expansion of their opportunities and the pursuit of high-level achievements.

Most of these eight groupings of strategies mentioned above are positively related to measures of happiness. The more you pursue social interaction or the achievement of goals, for example, the more likely you are to report higher levels of experience—though with one notable exception. Mental control, that is, avoiding thinking about being unhappy or what is wrong, cultivating a bright outlook, going to the movies alone, and taking illegal drugs, is negatively associated with experiential measures of happiness. These relations are interesting though we need to be particularly cautious about the possible directions of causality here. For one thing, it could be that mental control strategies don't work and make people unhappy but equally it could be that those who are unhappy turn to mental control as a tactic for lifting themselves out of their unhappy state. To get a better understanding of the relative balance, we would need either to conduct a controlled experiment or to follow what happens when happiness or strategies are dramatically affected by some external factor, so it would be premature to conclude that mental control is ineffective.

Another reason to be cautious about these findings concerns the fact that there are important differences between people, for example between genders and cultures. While both sexes were equally happy, men reported more frequent use of active leisure and mental control strategies. Women, by contrast, tended to be involved more frequently in social affiliation, goal pursuit, passive leisure, and religion. In addition, and compared with Asian students, white students reported greater involvement in partying and active leisure and less involvement in activities classified as passive leisure or mental control. Some sociologists have suggested that individualistic cultures have a tendency to promote high-arousal strategies in the pursuit of wellbeing and these results would seem to support that view. However, the key point is that because people are not homogenous we should be cautious when drawing inferences about simple relations between strategies and happiness. If an intervention, for example, were designed to increase opportunities for those who showed particularly low levels of socializing, it would need to be based on a good understanding of the causes and reasons for low levels of social interaction.

To conclude, and without trying to summarize these psychologically-oriented ways in which we might think about wellbeing, I suggest that a range of social issues, which for the most part don't show up in data on national income, are rather central to quality of life. That said, there is still an ethical aspect, to do with rights, justice, and fairness, that makes an essential contribution to human wellbeing and so it is to these issues that we now turn.

CHAPTER 7

FAIRNESS AND JUSTICE

Fairness in economic analysis used to be something of an optional extra: there was little agreement about how legitimate or significant it was and efficiency was what mattered. In fact it used to be thought that there was a trade-off between fairness and efficiency so that the price of justice might well be efficiency. But there is a problem of internal inconsistency with this traditional view. If people have preferences that are concerned about inequality, then unfair societies should, in theory, be regarded as inefficient by virtue of their failing to satisfy our preferences for fairness!

Today, there is a widespread recognition that fairness, justice, and related features of social arrangements are important contributors to the quality of the environments in which we live and work. In part this reflects the fact that many countries around the world now contribute meaningfully to the analysis of global issues through both their own educational systems as well as the major international organizations such as the World Bank and the United Nations to which they belong. But this growing concern with inequality also reflects the contributions of philosophical theorizing, especially those of Harvard philosopher John Rawls who nearly fifty years ago constructed a theory of justice using ideas from economic analysis that has helped to put these issues well and truly on the world's political and intellectual agendas.

Human reactions to unfairness underwrite the institutions of justice. A sense of fairness starts to emerge very early on in life, while anger and indignation at wrongful acts can be the most powerful of motives. In what follows, therefore, I want to look at evidence showing how fairness contributes to wellbeing through both personal experience as well as the success of collective endeavours, and I shall highlight the importance of distributive and procedural aspects which come together in Rawls' theory as well human flourishing.

Philosophical Preliminaries

Like many of the greatest philosophers, John Rawls was interested in constructing a theory that would help us to understand what justice could be and what implications this might have for the design of a fair society. His was an ethical theory in the sense that it was concerned with the wellbeing of people, but it was also a distributive theory concerned about the wellbeing of those least well-off in society.

In trying to work out how a society could be justly organized, Rawls suggested that we consider what reasonable people would choose if they knew all the significant facts about each position in society, but nothing about who would get which position. This provocative thought experiment he described as choosing from behind a veil of ignorance and he supposed that, in such a situation, rational individuals would be risk-averse. That is, people would choose, on the basis of self-interest, an egalitarian society that did as well, for the worst off, as possible just in case they ended up in that position themselves.

The theory is interesting for many reasons not least of which is the fact that it relies on a clear distinction between distributive and procedural forms of fairness. The distribution of the primary goods in society that emerges from the account is egalitarian. The veil of ignorance, by contrast, is a procedural mechanism for ensuring that people start on a level playing field. This particular theory argues that rational agents choosing through a fair process would agree to setting up a society that was fair—and egalitarian—in its distribution of outcomes. The theory provides some essential concepts for thinking about justice but to what extent does it reflect the way that fairness contributes to human wellbeing?

Evidence From The Ultimatum Game

Economics has, in practice, tended to assume that people are most concerned about their own financial gains and would be rather indifferent to issues of fairness but evidence from experiments conducted by economists now offers a rather different story: one such experiment often used in this context is known as the 'ultimatum game'. Typically, the game has two players who are given the opportunity to share $50, say. The first player proposes a distribution which the second player can either accept or reject. If accepted, the proposed distribution is made but if the second player rejects the proposal, then both players receive nothing. What do you predict the players will do and how would you play the game if you were one of them?

Considerations of self-interest alone predict that the first player should propose to keep $49, and to offer $1 to the other player. The second player has, in effect, a choice between $1, and nothing, and so should according to monetary considerations alone choose to accept the offer. The experiment has been replicated many times but the extremely unequal distribution is rarely observed. Typically second players prefer nothing to low and highly unequal offers, which they tend to reject. Anticipating this on the basis of intuitions about human nature, it would seem, proposals are often made by the first player, somewhere in the $10 to $25 range. Equal, or near equal, offers are much more frequently accepted.

It seems we find offers that are particularly unequal, and without any particular justification beyond self-interest, sufficiently unattractive that we are willing to punish the proposer of such offers even if doing so comes at a cost. The literature on these experiments is now vast and sophisticated but the simple, core insight remains intact. There is as yet no single, accepted account of what drives these results but a number of explanations have been offered. It has, for example, been shown that under certain circumstances people are simply averse to inequalities. According to the inequality aversion hypothesis, the proposals of the first player reflect not only self-interest but also a concern to avoid excessive disparities between the final outcomes.

A second line of argument contends that intentions matter. The proposer may wish to signal a desire to be reasonably fair thereby giving the second player a reason to accept the offer. It could be that there is some residue of reciprocal thinking going on in which the proposer considers how she or he would like to be treated if the roles were to be reversed. Whatever the mechanism, a huge volume of experiments show that very unequal distributions are generally not made and tend to be rejected when they are.

Fairness and Biology

There is growing evidence that fairness in experiments such as the ultimatum game is not so much perceived like a number or colour but rather that people derive an almost aesthetic pleasure in situations that are fair and an almost visceral feeling of disgust towards those that are not. In games such as the ultimatum game above, highly unequal offers generate activity in the anterior insula, a part of the brain related to basic survival needs such as taste, but also, in primates, to higher-level abilities such as the capacity to empathize: the greater the activity in this part of the brain, the more likely a person is to reject an offer.

Distributive fairness, is seems, has a connection to empathy and it can be asked whether these effects are distinct from those derived from financial pay-offs. As it happens, in a game examining the role of trust, deciding to punish a selfish opponent has been shown to be associated with greater activity in the caudate nucleus. This area of the brain is known to process rewards for goal-directed actions and the implication seems to be that internal thought processes can indeed reward the punishment of unfairness, even when there is no financial gain. This phenomenon has been found in other contexts and can be sensitive to gender. In another study for example, subjects were asked to play opponents in an ultimatum game who were either fair or unfair. In the second part of the experiment their empathy for former partners, who subjects were led to believe had received some discomfort, was measured. In the case of partners who had made fair offers, both men and women exhibited increased activity in the insular and anterior singulate regions, suggesting an empathetic response to the partner's pain. However, when men watched previous proposers of unfair offers (appear to) suffer discomfort, there was increased activity in reward areas of the brain—such as the ventral striatum. Judgements of fairness and our gut reactions would appear to be closely linked though it is worth observing that in a competition, anger is a better predictor of how people will respond compared with judgements of unfairness.

A sense of fairness in humans seems, then, to be connected to our ability to achieve desirable outcomes in some competitive, social settings, integral to the way we think and is not unique to humans. In an investigation using a version of the ultimatum game, non-human primates were trained to understand that a particular food token would yield an equal division of food whereas another would result in a five-to-one division in favour of the proposer. Proposers were allowed to choose a token and passed it on to the responder. The responder could then decide whether to accept the proposal and if they did, they would give it to the experimenter who would implement the proposal. Typically responders never rejected the offer made, even when low, but interestingly proposers nonetheless shifted over time from the uneven division to the even one. Once the proposer's own needs are met, there is room, it seems, for fairness and similar results have been found in experiments with young children.

There has also been some research using an 'impunity' game which is similar in structure to the ultimatum game above with the exception that if the responder rejects the offer, the proposer still receives their proposed share of the reward. In general, the evidence shows that non-human primates are more likely to refuse completing the task when the proposed distribution of food rewards is unequal. Moreover, there is some evidence that refusals are linked to effort and desert: unfair offers tend to be accepted if food is given out freely, but rejected if the food reward depends on contributions to the completion of a task.

Given the widespread evidence of a costly willingness to reject unfair distributions, it has been suggested this might be a mechanism for identifying good partners for collaborative tasks. One experiment that explored this possibility involved pairs of capuchin monkeys that received food pay-offs of differing levels of desirability if they were able to repeatedly pull heavy trays successfully. When the recipient of the more desired food item shared access to it, co-operative success was relatively high and took place in about 70 per cent of the completed tasks. In the partnerships where food rewards differed, but access to the more preferred item was not shared, co-operation occurred in only 30 per cent of the tasks. So it would seem that non-human primates can extrapolate across multiple interactions to signal and co-ordinate their willingness to collaborate and that fair distributions do indeed help to promote successful collaboration.

Procedural Justice, Equality of Opportunity, and the Experience of Discrimination

Even if we are ultimately concerned about the fair distribution of outcomes, there are several reasons why we might be interested in the fairness of the procedures used to achieve those outcomes. Not least is the fact that where people have different preferences or their interests conflict, the quality of the decision-making procedure might be something on which society at large can more easily agree. Just processes are central to politics and law and our current institutions reflect the evolution and refinement of these mechanisms over several millennia. Even so, our attitudes to procedural fairness, particularly the areas where we expect it to apply, are still changing significantly as principles such as 'equality of opportunity' and transparency illustrate. It is natural, therefore to ask, what do we mean by procedural fairness and how does it impact on our happiness and wellbeing?

In an earlier study of procedures as they operate in economics transactions, Daniel Kahneman and colleagues looked at the way in which people react to firms raising prices of snow-shovels the morning after a large storm. Prices might be expected to rise in order to equalize demand to the available supply but when the price hikes are high, people can often judge such behaviour as unfair. In their experiment with American consumers, the researchers found that more than 80 per cent of respondents judged opportunistic pricing in situations such as this to be unfair. So fairness has an impact on how people feel about market exchange and further evidence shows that procedural concerns are also important for public involvement in democratic political processes. In a study of 6000 adults, that exploited the regional variation of public involvement across the cantons of Switzerland, Bruno Frey and Alois Stutzer found that the greater the political participation rights are of a region's population, controlling for a range of factors including household income, the higher was their life satisfaction. In a related vein, a series of studies looking at the siting of waste-processing facilities with negative aesthetic, noise, and health risk impacts has found that offering direct financial compensation to local communities can be interpreted as a form of bribery and is often counterproductive as a result, even though it might, in theory, appear to be an efficient form of compensation. Rather, it seems that if an airport brings with it road congestion and noise, local residents are more likely to accept proposals that directly address the potential harms done such as traffic control measures or improvements to the sound insulation of houses and workplaces, than they are a sum of money.

The importance of treating people fairly has been studied also in legal contexts where acceptance of judicial action depends not just on what is done but also the ways that individuals are treated leading up to a decision. Work by Edgar Lind and colleagues, for example, shows that in arbitration-based awards, litigants who judge the process to be fair are much more likely to accept the decision, regardless of its outcome. Elsewhere, it has been found that courteous treatment by arresting officers of perpetrators in domestic violence incidents can lead to a reduction in subsequent reoffending rates. We might take procedural fairness for granted in many situations but perhaps we should be more open to the scope that it has, in a range of settings, for helping people achieve acceptable outcomes.

Outside of research, arguably one of the most significant changes in attitudes to procedural fairness over the past half century around the world concerns the espousal of equal opportunity principles in the workplace as applied to sex, ethnicity, and a range of other criteria. Few democratic politicians can afford the luxury of ignoring half of their potential voters while in business, as Gary Becker has pointed out, companies are forced in competitive market situations to look for the most appropriate productive workers regardless of their personal identities.

Under the broad heading of gender equality are issues concerned with economic discrimination, gender-based violence, health in equal-ities, and traditional cultural practices considered inappropriate by virtue of their attendant harms or risks. For the purposes of international comparisons, the Global Gender Gap Index constructed by Harvard economist Ricardo Hausmann provides an interesting source of data. The intention is to measure outcomes related to basic rights by measuring differences between women and men in four areas: health, education, economic participation, and political empowerment. Policies, culture, and customs are excluded from the index on the grounds that they should best be regarded as inputs. Health and education are measured in relatively standard ways, while the economic component of the index includes measures of participation in the workforce, wage equality for similar work, women in senior government and business positions, and a measure of women in professional and technical roles. Political empowerment is measured using numbers of seats in parliament and ministerial-level appointments held by women as well as the number of female heads of state over the past fifty years. According to the index, in 2012, out of

135 countries, the U.K. was ranked 18th, U.S.A. 22nd, Germany 13th, France 57th, and Ireland 5th. The top three countries were Scandinavian while the bottom three were spread across the Middle East and western Asia. Within the lowest-income country grouping, Mozambique and Burundi were ranked highest. It is also noticeable that the preponderance of resource-rich states towards the lower end of Hausmann's index could indicate that such countries are shielded, in part, from competitive forces that might otherwise help to reduce gender disparities.

While higher national income is weakly associated with reductions in the gender gap, there appears to be a stronger connection with a country's culture, history, and geography. In all low-, middle-, and high-income country groups, it is possible to find countries with very different levels of gender equity and insofar as comparisons can be made, the gaps appear smallest in health and educational attainment, largest for political empowerment, with economic participation falling somewhere in between. In the seven years since the index was developed, no domain has worsened, though only political participation has improved to a degree that is noticeable. Hausmann's index and its movement over time might be taken to suggest that women around the world share the prospect of a global glass ceiling which in turn raises the question as to why such ceilings are so persistent and difficult to break through.

One explanation developed by economists at Bristol University proposes that such barriers can be the result of normal business competition combined with the fact that women have more attractive alternative options outside of the workplace, compared to men. The basic idea behind their economic model is that employers don't have perfect information about the future productivity of each individual at work so make judgements based on what they know about the average characteristics of workers. Even if men and women are statistically identical with respect to their characteristics relevant to work, women have different home-based options to men. These simple and plausible assumptions turn out to be a major problem for those women who are as committed to employment as their male counterparts. To be promoted, such women need to signal their commitment to their employment and may choose to work harder as a way of doing this. If such additional effort is not easily observed by competing firms, a company might still just offer harder-working women the going rate and the result is that even if not discriminated against directly, women might nevertheless have to work harder than male counterparts to achieve similar outcomes.

Different models can come to different conclusions based on variations in their assumptions but Bristol's model helps to make a crucial point. Legislation requiring gender neutral contracts might have no impact on gender inequality whereas making career breaks more attractive to men or imposing quotas on promotions are approaches that could be effective. It remains an open question whether either option would be politically attractive but the model does help to demonstrate the fact that ensuring fair and equal treatment in reality may require a lot more analysis of behaviour and incentives than merely just passing a law that makes it obligatory.

While the bases of discrimination are relatively immobile for sex, race, and to some extent material poverty, as an experience it can take many forms. People can be socially excluded by being ignored, can be stigmatized and stereotyped through verbal or non-verbal interactions, and acts of discrimination can vary from a tacit reduction in expectations through to threats of physical violence or damage to property. The phenomenological aspects of discrimination are salient, can literally be in your face, and are not things to which people adapt: indeed there is evidence that these experiences are connected to psychological distress, depression, and high blood pressure.

A number of different psychological reactions have been identified and studied. A person might, for example, seek to develop a strong identity as a buffer—one theory being that a strong internal sense of value can help protect or override negative views from external sources. Evidence on the effectiveness of this strategy, however, is mixed and suggests that for some (not all) groups, the approach is of little value. An alternative strategy is to seek and develop support through social networks, confidants or professional advisers. Such support is known to benefit physical and psychological health though the evidence for effectiveness is, again, mixed, as some supporting activities can be counterproductive if the negative events are more salient. It is tempting to think that direct expressions of anger and frustration may be helpful and there is some evidence that this is associated with dwelling less on incidents after they have happened. All that said, in her assessment of the psychological research, Elizabeth Brondolo concludes that evidence of efficacy of all these strategies is weak.

In summary, both distributive and procedural fairness matter to people and constitute an integral part of human wellbeing. This is true both in terms of experiences as well as entitlements, which are clearly connected though in ways that are complex. Societies may have difficulties getting priorities right, sorting out important entitlements from frivolous claims, but there seems little doubt that we have preferences for penalizing injustices, particularly those that under-mine personal dignity and collective action. Evidence on the use of psychological coping mechanisms does not support the view that people easily adapt to these problems and therefore suggests that if societies want to promote and maintain fairness for all, they need to ensure that appropriate institutional structures, education, and incentives are in place.

CHAPTER 8

INTERNATIONAL AND POLICY PERSPECTIVES

In this penultimate chapter, I want to consider the extent to which any of this research on happiness and wellbeing has an impact on policy or practice? The question is beginning to be asked and of course in a sense governments and charities already exist to improve the wellbeing of citizens. However, there is a slightly different emphasis deriving from research and policy experience over the past two or three decades which is difficult to encapsulate exactly but centres around a new unwillingness to accept that, with the exception of deep poverty, an exclusive focus on income may not be enough to maximize people's wellbeing. There is less evidence on use in practice and so in this chapter I offer a small collection of case-studies, some drawing on personal experience, that illustrate the kinds of developments that are emerging.

Bhutan and Gross National Happiness

Many countries around the world are now interested in life quality, as distinct from income, and at least some of this interest derives from a throw-away comment made by the King of Bhutan who in 1972 suggested that his country might do better to measure Gross National Happiness (GNH) rather than Gross Domestic Product. Bhutan is a small rural country with a predominantly Bhuddhist population, balanced on the foothills of the Himalayas, and over the past couple of decades has developed a distinctive approach to government planning based on principles that are resonant with its historical traditions.

As a result it was one of the first countries in the world to develop a set of high-profile indicators that would provide an alternative to GDP and help monitor progress in terms of non-financial priorities.

The indicators Bhutan has chosen are founded on religious and cultural values and have nine dimensions comprising psychological wellbeing, time-use (sufficient time for non-work activities), community vitality, culture (diversity and resilience of traditions), health, education, environment, living standards, and governance (perceptions of equity honesty and quality). The list reflects the country's own priorities but it contains many elements that would be of concern to populations in any country and illustrates one way in which a country can develop its own alternative vision of how progress should be monitored.

Moreover, these ideas have been influential within central government where the planning unit has developed a screening tool based on twenty-two criteria against which all new policies are scored. Policies must reach a threshold value to be acceptable and occasionally have been referred back to ministries for revision when this was not the case.

The approach has not been free from criticism. The incoming Prime Minister in 2013, for example, expressed concern about the balance of impact between international audiences and local populations, arguing that national debt from the main hydro-electric projects was a significant issue that GNH could not address. GDP growth rates have been high in recent years by international standards—between 5 per cent and 7 per cent—and yet migration to urban centres is giving rise to significant underemployment particularly among the young where unemployment rates have touched 30 per cent. The co-existence of rapid GDP growth, high unemployment, and high levels of debt is perhaps not a unique problem for developing countries and one that serves to highlight precisely why focusing exclusively on monetary indicators of progress isn't always sufficient to promote human wellbeing on a sustainable basis.

Sometimes non-governmental projects and organizations can play a role in shaping the nature and development of economic activity and one notable example is the Loden foundation's entrepreneurship scheme designed to help new businesses create employment. The scheme acts as a business incubator, providing mentoring and loans (free and without collateral) to a handful of new business proposers each year. Most business activities are eligible—though they should be consistent with local cultural, environmental, and religious values—and each entrepreneur is given access (usually online) to a mentoring panel comprising experts in different areas of business advice. Almost all ventures supported are successful and there have been examples of business operators offering to make donations back to the foundations as a result. There are, no doubt, many such somewhat similar schemes around the world but the scheme helps to illustrate how it is possible to develop economic activity in a way that integrates and incorporates human development in to it.

The Danes Have A Word For It

The Danish word for happiness, *hygge* (pronounced roughly huy-gah), is also translated as 'cosy' and for a few years now surveys have suggested that people in Denmark are the happiest on the planet. Indeed other Scandinavian countries also do rather well so one might ask what it is about these countries that leads to such high levels of satisfaction with life? From the 1960s on, Denmark has been known as an early mover in the global liberalization of attitudes towards social relations but it is a wealthy country and there are other factors at work also. For one thing, it has a relatively homogenous culture and enjoys low crime rates. These things often go together, and both have positive impacts not only on experience but also on the activities that people are able to undertake. Approximately 90 per cent of the country's population are ethnically Danish and the shared values, history and religion helps government, it has been argued, to understand the preferences of its population. Such environments are conducive to the development of trust and indeed these are relatively high there.

A second set of issues arises from the fact that inequalities are low and government policies appear to give an important role to families that go beyond working out how best to tax families, important as this is. Parents are entitled to substantial amounts of maternity and paternity leave to look after their children starting with a year of leave shared by the mother and father. The educational system, which came first in the UN's global Education Index in 2010, is also of interest by virtue of the emphasis it places on students taking responsibility for making good decisions themselves. Primary schools emphasize attendance, participation and progress—but not exams— and teachers are seen as facilitators of children's learning rather than responsible for maximizing test results. Secondary schools, likewise, emphasize pupil interest and use it to broaden mindsets while offering activities that enable students to develop their own cognitive and social skills.

National disposition, it has been suggested, also plays a part in Denmark's apparent success. With a population of around 5 million, it is a small peaceful country with little interest in world dominance. Danes enjoy a high standard of living, but they also seem to have a good quality of life depending on the measures used. Compared with Americans who report higher levels of both positive and negative feelings, the Danes report higher levels of satisfaction and enjoyment. Furthermore, and perhaps more important, those in the bottom income group experience less negative satisfaction than their counterparts in other countries. So notwithstanding the contributions of Denmark's own unique history, a number of contemporary social, economic, and educational facts and policies would seem to be the basis for the population's overall wellbeing. Work–life balance, autonomy, social factors and a somewhat egalitarian ethos may all be things from which we can learn even if they are difficult to replicate, for economic or political reasons, in larger countries.

National Wellbeing in the U.K.

Work on wellbeing as a distinct focus of central government thinking in the U.K. has been ongoing for several years under a variety of parties and, by 2014, at least forty-three separate policies, programmes or areas of service delivery had been evaluated in terms of their capacity to benefit from a wellbeing perspective. In government reports, these initiatives are seen as work in progress and the emphasis is not so much on developing new areas of government policy to promote happiness as refining the mechanisms by which policies can include human wellbeing more explicitly rather than focusing solely on financial pathways.

One example can be found in work by the Department for Business Innovation and Skills (BIS) for example, which spends over £200m each year on community learning—a range of courses from arts through family learning and healthy living to using a computer. Evaluations of this work were published in 2012 and they showed that adult learning has significant impacts on life satisfaction and health including mental health. Estimates suggest that on average an adult learning course leads to an increase in life satisfaction equivalent to something in the region of an additional £750 to £950 in income: adult learners in the 50 to 69 age range benefit significantly as do those with low basic skills. In an evaluation of some 4000 community learners commissioned by BIS, 89 per cent of learners reported that their course helped them keep mind and body active, 81 per cent that the course made them feel better about themselves generally, and 75 per cent that it helped them relax or get a break from everyday stress. These findings have shaped BIS's approach to community learning.

In 2011, the U.K. piloted and subsequently launched a National Citizen Service programme that provides an opportunity for young people to develop social and community interests. The scheme is voluntary and open to 16 and 17 year olds who attend a residential activity centre before taking part in a community-based project, which is then awarded a certificate on completion. An early-stage, independent evaluation has found positive impacts in terms of communication, teamwork, leadership, and the transition to adulthood. Furthermore, the majority of participants, though not all, felt the experience enjoyable, worthwhile, and provided an opportunity to mix with young people from different strata in society with whom they would not normally come into contact.

A couple of years later, a major reform to the delivery of public health was introduced with the remit of improving wellbeing across the life course and raising awareness of lifestyle challenges and other causes of health inequality. The approach has led to some interesting headlines in the newspapers such as one asking should fishing rods be available on prescription? A group of doctors in the North of England that took an early interest in the wellbeing perspective to health care has already developed three streams of wellbeing services. One involves direct referral to a community wellbeing officer who takes a life history, seeks to understand a person's difficulties and helps to develop, where appropriate, options for recovery. A second comprises what is referred to as social prescribing and in the main focuses on the development of life skill courses which are generally free and targeted at those in the most deprived areas. The third strand of more general events and initiatives tries to encourage flourishing in a positive sense and has included general practice innovations that have ranged from tango dancing to Nordic walking for the elderly.

There is also some evidence that legislation is beginning to be influenced by this agenda. It is now, by law, possible for employees to ask for flexible working arrangements and there are new guidelines which encourage town planners and architects to factor into the design of public spaces an allowance for, and the encouragement of, physical social interactions. Administrative practices are changing also with the Cabinet Office offering spending departments a workshop on how ideas and evidence about wellbeing can inform policy design. The pattern that is emerging seems not to be one of the evolution of major spending programmes but rather the development of a range of initiatives that are modest in cost but nonetheless might make a difference to people's lives, especially to those with particular needs they find difficult to address without assistance.

Australia

Work by the Australian government offers another example of practical engagement with happiness and wellbeing, in this case one explicitly grounded in the account of human flourishing outlined earlier. Developed as a framework to help civil servants bring wellbeing into the design of policy, it has a number of elements to it. Firstly, it highlights the importance of opportunities available to people, not just in terms of goods and services but including also 'good health and environmental amenity, leisure and intangibles such as personal and social activities, community participation and political rights and freedoms'. Further, the framework is concerned about the distribution of these goods to the extent that everyone has 'the opportunity to lead a fulfilling life and participate meaningfully in society'. And finally, it emphasizes the question of how sustainable these opportunities are over time and the importance attached to the overall level and allocation of risks borne by individuals as opposed to society at large.

This approach has been used in a number of applications including the education of staff about the objectives of public policy, signalling externally government recognition that human wellbeing is not just a matter of finance helping staff to engage with external stakeholders. It is viewed by Treasury as a conceptual tool that addresses some of the limits of traditional policy analysis and emphasizes economic activity as an instrument for the promotion of wellbeing throughout the population. Other approaches to happiness can be found in Australia but the emphasis on opportunities, distributional fairness, and subjective experience provides a valuable example of how core relations and concepts of the human flourishing framework can be used in policy.

Mexico

There has been considerable policy interest in the human flourishing across Latin America and since at least 2006 Mexico has been developing, at national level, a system for measuring wellbeing using a multi-dimensional approach. The country's approach is shared by other countries in the region and emphasizes the importance of social rights and a keen interest in understanding and supporting those who are least well off in these terms, in many cases indigenous people living in the south of the country. The Mexican government is required by its own laws to monitor a range of aspects of quality of life including income per head, educational problems, access to health services, access to social security, quality of living spaces, housing, access to basic services, access to food as well as the level of what it calls 'social cohesion'. The approach is used to identify three groups—those in extreme poverty, the poor, and those vulnerable to falling below the poverty threshold. To identify who is poor, thresholds for each dimension are specified so that people who fall below the threshold are defined as being deprived on those dimensions. As a result, it is possible to see not just those who are on incomes below a given threshold but to develop a more detailed picture which shows, for example, that over 40 per cent of the population have insufficient access to health services, that nearly 20 per cent have no access to social security, and between 15 per cent and 20 per cent do not have access to adequate housing and associated services.

Using these data, the government has considered how different policies might help not only alleviate actual extreme deprivation but also protect those at risk of falling into poverty. Moreover it views job creation and economic growth as mechanisms for raising income and sees policies for health, education, and housing, what it calls social policies, as important mechanisms by which non-income deprivations can be reduced. This multi-dimensional approach has led the government to consider a variety of policies, at least some of which it regards as promoting social cohesion by requiring non-discrimination.

Some policies are targeted at the poor whereas others, for example to do with social security, health, and growth, are universal in that they are designed to improve the wellbeing of all. In practice, the government has found that the approach is helping social programmes to identify who their beneficiaries are, and who they should be. A number of government departments have developed an understanding of how their activities can contribute to the improvement of population wellbeing in poorer regions, while in central government the approach is being used to evaluate policies both before and after implementation.

Policies that lift the opportunities of those at the bottom are not always as easy to identify as one might hope but one that has shown some promising results is Mexico's Oportunidades Program. Designed around the fact that the poor make low-level investments in the education and health of their children, a conditional cash transfer programme transfers financial support to selected households, conditional on them improving their levels of human development. For keeping children enrolled in secondary school, monthly grants of £6 for boys and £40 for girls are offered where the difference reflects the fact that girls are more like to drop out early from school. A further grant of about £10 a month is available to improve food consumption and nutrition for toddlers, malnourished preschool-aged children, and women who are breast-feeding or pregnant.

This programme was designed by experienced senior government officials with presidential support and has had a programme of external evaluation built in from the outset. Households are selected for inclusion using geographical data (used to estimate family means) and grants are paid to mothers as evidence indicates that they make best use of the funds. An early evaluation has shown that primary school enrolments rose by 10 per cent for boys and 20 per cent for girls, that children between 1–5 years had a 12 per cent less chance of illness compared with children in the control group, and that the growth rates of children between 1 and 3 years who received treatment increased by some 16 per cent.

Following these favourable evaluations the programme has been extended in coverage to include the urban poor and engage with secondary school children. Economic modelling has not only shown that the programme does indeed serve to increase enrolment rates at the end of primary school but also that offering more resources to older children and less to younger ones could keep even more children at school until leaving age.

Mexican NGOs also have been interested in the approach and one (known locally as Yoquiero-yopuedo 'I want to I can') has developed a series of skills development workshops for those particularly disadvantaged. Over a hundred thousand Mexicans have benefited from its programmes which cover topics ranging from job training and substance abuse to broaching difficult topics with parents, and asking questions in class. Workshops are designed to be participatory and reflective as a way of focusing on the development of skill, rather than the mastery of knowledge. The guiding philosophy is that, in addition to focusing on a particular issue, the generic skills developed can be used in other contexts. The Mexican NGO calls this a psychosocial approach to empowerment and its work highlights the contribution of core decision-making and social skills to the development of an active community that can effect change, rather than be its victim.

The Better Life Index

One of the challenges for happiness and wellbeing concerns the deceptively simple issue of presenting and summarizing information on the wide range of factors that contribute to happiness and wellbeing. The OECD has done a lot of work in this area, much of which has revolved around the development of a dashboard of indicators informed by the human flourishing framework. Its work parallels closely my team's research and employs an interactive website, used now by over a million people, to show how different aspects of wellbeing vary between countries and how different sets of priorities serve to rank countries differently.

The OECD's Better Life Compendium, produced first in 2011, provided a public launch pad for this work which seeks to distinguish clearly between material living conditions—a traditional focus of economics—and quality of life, which covers non-monetary issues and the sustainability of socio-economic and natural systems. The index itself contains data for all its member states on income and wealth, jobs and earnings, housing, health status, work–life balance, education and skills, civic engagement and governance, social connections, environmental quality, personal security, and subjective wellbeing.

Unlike most indices, where value weights are predefined, the OECD index allows people to create country- and issue-based rankings using their own relative valuations. Often the ranking of a country will change significantly as different aspects of life quality are given more or less weight. The life quality data used to drive the Better Life Index can also be used to provide snapshots of how individual countries are doing in terms of human wellbeing. An evaluation of wellbeing in the U.K. since the 2008 financial crisis, for example, shows that *average* households in all four constituent countries were only affected moderately by the event but that there were more noticeable impacts on jobs, life satisfaction, and civic engagement. Over the period 2007 to 2011 trust in institutions increased significantly, though this was in stark contrast to other OECD countries where it declined markedly. Countries most impacted by the crisis have experienced notable increases in civic engagement—for example volunteering—though no such trend was found in the U.K. Some of these findings are not always as might be expected and provide support for the view that we should not assume that social and economic changes are always closed related.

This chapter has provided only a handful of examples of ways in which happiness and human flourishing are being reflected in policy and practice. They come from different areas and issues in policy but what, one may ask, links this new wave of initiatives. If earlier interest was associated with the development of social indicators in the 1970s, then this second wave shares with it a basic concern about the limitations of GDP as a measure of human wellbeing but seems to take the issue further in terms of concepts, methods, and even ambitions for policy and practice. Measurement is essential if governments are to take the issue seriously but equally it is what we do with these data that counts and, in Chapter 9, I shall elaborate further what individuals and societies might do in this regard.

PROGRESS AS HUMAN DEVELOPMENT

Though human flourishing was developed as a constructive response to problems that lie at the intersection of economics and philosophy, it provides a theory of happiness and wellbeing consistent with much of what we know empirically from psychology, health and social science. We might assume that money is related to happiness and wellbeing but this raises questions about the nature and extent of the relation. What does happiness and wellbeing change over the life course? How should we think about money on the one hand, and the final outcomes that we hope it will help us achieve? What are the implications of human diversity? Human flourishing offers a framework that allows such questions to be posed and addressed: it was born from concerns about the omission of rights from utilitarianism and welfare economics and its structure focuses on the many different dimensions of happiness and wellbeing, their drivers, and the fact that there are significant differences between individuals. The activities and opportunities we value vary over the life course but there are, nonetheless, some themes that endure throughout and here I want to mention four.

Four Underlying Principles

The fact that we are social animals, generally living and working in multiple *communities* of different sizes and configurations clearly has consequences for happiness and wellbeing, though this simple point has not had the emphasis in some areas of policy that it deserves.

Social skills, in addition to the cognitive skills developed through education and training, are increasingly important in the work place and the evidence is that these benefit significantly from things that take place very early on in life. At the other end of the age spectrum, having daily face-to-face contact with friends and family is also important. Despite living on a crowded planet, the risks of isolation and loneliness are real and substantial.

We also value *autonomy* both for ourselves and for those we care about though the balance between independence and reliance changes dramatically throughout life and is shaped by many diverse events and experiences. We help children become self-sufficient as they grow, while at the end of life we are concerned that a person's wishes be respected. How autonomy is expressed varies enormously depending on our potential and what we want to do with it. There are many forms of self-expression from the creations of artistic genius to the development of a personal identity and this gives rise to a difficult balancing act. Autonomy requires the freedom to act but also a willingness to accept norms that facilitate living in a society with others who may hold different views or wish to pursue different projects.

Closely related, though often in the background is, as we have seen, the concept of *fairness*. Concerns about distributive fairness are deeply rooted and there is no reason to believe that the world will necessarily evolve in a manner that is fair—fairness is not a good or service we can very easily buy in a shop (or online for that matter). We do have an ingrained capacity to react when treated unfairly which in turn suggests we have good reason to be concerned about the growing polarization of societies.

Finally, it has been argued that happiness and wellbeing depends importantly on a person's *engagement* with life. The concept of flow is particularly relevant here and as with the previous three issues it seems to have a relevance for us across the life span. For young children, participation across a range of activities is important in their development and is often used to assess their levels of engagement while in older age failure to engage in social activities is a known predictor of death. Engagement is associated with a cluster of related terms such as zest, vitality, interest, and with other aspects of experience: different people and cultures no doubt have different optimal levels but nonetheless, significant disengagement at any age is potentially a cause for concern.

These four elements, fairness, autonomy, community, and engagement (FACE) are fundamental contributors to happiness and wellbeing throughout life but they may also sit at the centre of many potential and actual conflicts. We live at a time when we are increasingly related to each other as much by what we can know about others as any formal distinctions or barriers that might keep people apart. As a result, our happiness and wellbeing has a global aspect to it and may depend on others who seem remote and irrelevant to us. Bearing in mind these principles, what might we do to sustain or improve human wellbeing?

What Can Individuals Do For Themselves...

Any study of happiness inevitably leads to questions about what individuals and societies should do and here I have identified and discussed some evidence and concepts that could inform any attempt to answer such questions. There are, of course, many lists and books of things that individuals should do if they want to improve their own happiness and wellbeing and one that is research-based has been produced by the charity Action for Happiness. Roughly its recommendations comprise two groups—one to do with actions and a second to do with the way we might think.

The activities it proposes include the following: doing things for others, expressing gratitude when grateful, seeking help when finding things difficult, helping your children develop emotional skills, volunteering time, energy, and skills, trying something new, helping a friend in need, getting enough sleep, listening to others, understanding the needs of those around you, getting to know your neighbours, asking others about things that have gone well, going outside and enjoying nature, taking a break from technology, making exercise enjoyable, making time for activities with family and friends, and looking for satisfaction at work. In addition to these actions, it proposes ways of thinking that might also be conducive to happiness and wellbeing including: looking for the good in those around you, being mindful, being curious, knowing your thoughts, developing positive thought patterns in favour of negative ones, being realistic, putting yourself in a positive frame of mind, finding strengths and focusing on using them, learning to mediate, and finding your purpose.

Such proposals are becoming widespread (there are many similar lists out there now) and while some relate to thought, many involve action which suggests that happiness is not all in the mind—even if the way we think and feel are essential contributors to, and constituents of, happiness. The majority of actions concern day-to-day activities while others imply actions that require sustained effort over a prolonged period. Some suggestions are aimed at promoting personal mental and physical health while others encourage the development of our prosocial sides. All are consistent with the human flourishing framework and the scientific research discussed in this book. They do not constitute a panacea for the world's intractable problems, but they offer us as individuals some concrete steps that can be taken to improve the quality of our own lives as well as the lives of those around us. The list has much to commend it but chances are people won't change just by reading about these things for the evidence shows that behaviour change is rarely a matter of just learning the relevant facts (as we see with decisions to quit smoking). For adults, the choice must surely ultimately be their own but when it comes to children the need to design educational curricula means we have to take a position on which skills are going to be valuable throughout life.

...and What Might Societies Do To Help?

If we elevate happiness and wellbeing in our thinking then some of the logic of basic, traditional ways of economic thinking becomes challengeable. A simple example concerns food which is increasingly not prepared at home. The use of time-saving prepared foods seems completely benign taken in isolation but doctors in Texas have also documented how it is contributing to a family lifestyle in which children eat alone, in their bedrooms, in front of their personal computer and TV screens. The reduction in parent–child interaction and transmission of knowledge, does not, their evidence suggests, have positive impacts on the children involved and it raises a question about how these negative social externalities of technological progress might be addressed. Somehow, we have to find ways of taking the good from technological change while at the same time minimizing the downsides.

Another issue that operates at the global level concerns the connections between free trade and decent work. Both of these are major international priorities, promoted and overseen by the World Trade Organization and International Labour Organization respectively, but trade and decent work are connected in ways that have yet to be reflected in the international agenda. In trade, the conventional wisdom is based on the work of the nineteenth-century economist David Ricardo who showed, roughly, that whenever two countries had different abilities in the production of goods, it would be beneficial for both to specialize and trade. However, if technology and trade combine in such a way that productive activity can be moved rapidly around the world to the lowest-cost producer at any one time, as is now the case for many consumer goods from jeans to laptops, then surely trade is also contributing to the instability of employment? As we noted in Chapter 5, economists have found that one of the major sources of unhappiness at work is uncertainty about continued employment in the future so it would seem that Ricardo's model needs to be expanded to include wellbeing derived from sources other than the consumption of goods, if we want to avoid deriving conclusions from it that are correct but misleading. An updated version would allow for the fact that people are, on average, averse both to risks and losses—that is a given loss will have more of a (negative) impact on a person than an equivalent gain would benefit them. So there might be a stability of employment argument for limits on free trade, rather like other health and safety limitations which we already now accept. Indeed some lower-income countries are currently arguing that in some circumstances completely free trade does not seem to be what they need. Without further evidence and analysis we won't know but at least we should try to find out. A happiness perspective does not encourage us to merely assume that the case for people as consumers always trumps the case for people as workers—we need at some point to look at the evidence.

We can also usefully think about society contributions to health and wellbeing from the perspective of what economists call 'market failure'. Typically, this occurs when markets provide too little or too much of a good compared with what people would like given the costs of producing the good or service in question. But it seems there are new kinds of market failures where the choice environment that evolves through market competition is not one that we would choose, if indeed we gave ourselves the choice. We live now, for example, in a world that, for most of us, is brimming with opportunities to eat but diminishing in the need for all the calories that can so conveniently be consumed. This seems to be a somewhat novel kind of market failure, one where competition leads to the development of a choice *environment* that is not necessarily optimal. At least human flourishing provides the possibility for assessing economic activity in terms of valued human outcomes.

Some have questioned whether we should in fact monitor wellbeing at the national level lest political actors use the information to manipulate our happiness to obtain our votes. But surely this is precisely what we want from our political representatives! Do we not want them to respond to human needs and issues as well as those of business? Elsewhere, others have argued that it is too early to design policies based on wellbeing and life satisfaction analyses and that more research is needed. The latter part of this view is nearly always true—there is always room for more research—but the first part, I suggest is overly pessimistic. In health, for example, there is a well-established tradition of designing and evaluating interventions to improve mental as well as physical health. In fact, as we have just seen in Chapter 8, the ideas of happiness and wellbeing are indeed being used to shape a range of practical initiatives in education, international development, and social protection.

At this stage, we surely do need to better understand the ways in which collective action might facilitate the pursuit of happiness and wellbeing or reduce the barriers that get in the way. The issue of how corporations treat us as workers provides a useful test case. Do we want to see, for example, more women on company boards, and/or more opportunities for equal opportunities and work–life balance? The evidence from around the world seems to be that many people want both things even if company law, in many cases, currently favours shareholders first and foremost. But it is perfectly possible to design and run companies in which the benefits of other stakeholders are predominant as the continued rise of the social enterprise illustrates.

Another line of argument offered against the monitoring of wellbeing is concerned that government interventions are illiberal. These concerns first emerged a couple of hundred years ago when the relations between individuals and governments were often characterized by remoteness and lack of information. However, today, we live and work in environments where corporations have researched extensively how they might most effectively entice the consumer away from their hard-earned dollars. If consumers are completely rational then there is no problem but in reality there is often a material, informational imbalance between people and the corporations from which they buy and, at the very least, we should be wary that this disparity does not create situations that fail, on balance, to improve human wellbeing.

Quality Of Life For All

In conclusion, I want to propose that, somewhat along the lines of Seneca, the evidence suggests happiness is a serious business which calls for much greater awareness and literacy about what we know. Not only will this help us be better decision-makers about our own happiness and wellbeing but it should help us contribute to debates about collective problems that can only be resolved at a societal level. Aspects of the life quality issues discussed here have entered the school curriculum at various points from lessons on domestic skills such as cookery, through sex-education to citizenship but there is undoubtedly room for much more.

An interesting example of what can be done exists at Wellington College, a school in the south of England that introduced, in 2006, a course on happiness and life quality aimed at 14 year olds. The College's curriculum has attracted considerable attention nationally and beyond and has replaced teaching previously described as personal, social, and health education. This new wellbeing programme comprises six strands—physical health, positive relationships, perspective (related particularly to resilience and thinking for coping with adversity), engagement, the world (particularly sustainability and personal relations to a materialistic world), and finally meaning and purpose.

Over the years, the school has developed a series of courses for 12–16 year olds that expand its curriculum to include drug awareness and misuse through to personal relations—the latter including an opportunity to interview a married couple about their relations in a classroom setting. In part, these courses are delivered by senior pupils and they cover topics ranging from the interpretation of behaviour and feelings through to developing strategies for thinking in different ways and self-awareness in order to control personal wellbeing. Classes involve the use of motivating issues, which might be a video clip, some skills training, and a period for evaluation that is reflected on in homework and receives comments from a teacher. Homework is not marked as the aim is to encourage students to develop their own reasoning rather than try to second-guess what the 'right' reason might be. The school also offers taster courses to parents, which have also proved very popular. Wellington's experience illustrates what is possible and is becoming an important guide for the development of school education in the U.K. Working and living in environments and societies where people are *literate* about the drivers of life quality could make such a difference to the world in which we live.

In closing, I hope this book helps to make the case that happiness in the broadest sense can, at the population level and to a useful degree, be defined, measured, explained, and enhanced. All of this is perfectly compatible with happiness at the individual level being a somewhat fragile, intangible thing best approached obliquely and autonomously. Wellbeing has many dimensions which vary in importance across the life course, as well as between individuals: it depends on our day-to-day social interactions with others, the events that happen to us, our internal experiences of these things, and also the opportunities that society makes available to us. I'd like to think, therefore, that we do now have a rough but workable idea of how to assess the quality of economic growth from a human perspective. If I were to allow myself one hedgehog thought, it would be just that if we want societies to prosper, their economies need to be socially sustainable in the sense of delivering happiness and wellbeing through communities that provide fairness, autonomy, society, and engagement. Human flourishing requires no less and it exciting to see schools and governments around the work responding to this emerging agenda.

ACKNOWLEDGEMENTS

This book would not have been possible without the thoughts, assistance and support of many people. I am indebted particularly to Amartya Sen whose work I first came across as a student in Oxford and then again when I edited a special issue of the Greek Economic Review to mark his 60th birthday. He has been very generous in supporting the theoretical and empirical projects that lie behind this book and that support has served as both an intellectual benchmark and source of inspiration and encouragement. My debts in the field have accumulated over the years and I particularly want to thank Enrico Giovannini, Richard Layard, Bruno Frey, Tony Addison, Clemens Puppe, Sudhir Anand, Marc Fleurbaey, Christophe Muller, Xavi Ramos, Avner Offer, Wulf Gaertner, Prasanta Pattanaik, Sabina Alkire, and Ian Crawford who have all made invaluable contributions to project conferences in Oxford and at OECD in Paris.

In addition, I am especially indebted to many colleagues with whom I have had the pleasures of working, especially Ron Smith, Keith Dowding, Martin van Hees, Ian Carter, Francesco Guala, Jaya Krishnakumar, Graham Hunter, Laurence Roope, Graciela Tonen, Cristina Santos, Dermot Coates, Paul Dolan, Andrew Clark, Iris Mantovani, Maria Sigala, Ian Bache, Louise Reardon, Alastair Gray, and James Heckman who also acted as an adviser to the Leverhulme Trust-funded research. I would also like to thank the inimitable Wolfsonian, Michael Argyle, who agreed to be a joint supervisor of Graham Hunter's thesis, but passed away early on in the project.

Some of the material has benefited from comments by seminar participants or at panel debates in a variety of institutions including the Kennedy School of Government at Harvard, the LBJ School of Government in Austin, Nuffield College Oxford, and the London School of Economics. Comments and encouragement from a number of people at these events have been numerous though I particularly want to mention Sarah Brown, Jenny Robertson, David Suckler, John Ermisch, Melinda Mills, Jonathan Wolff, Richard Bradley, and Stephen Lea. For discussions relating particularly to Chapter 8, I also need to thank a number of eminent practitioners in the field including Martine Durand, Ewan McKinnon, Eva Jespersen, Karma Tshiteem, Jonathan Hall, Susan Pick, Jeni Klugman, Marco Mira D'Ercole, Romina Boarini, Sarah Stewart-Brown Paul Alin and other ONS Task Force members, colleagues in Oxfam and Oxfam India, as well as those who have read the text including David Bartram, Martin Binder, and Rynn Reed.

Finally I must acknowledge a number of institutional debts including those owed to Wolfson College and what is now Green-Templeton College, in Oxford, as well as the Leverhulme Trust, the Arts and Humanities Research Council, the Economic and Social Research Council, the Open University, the Health Economics Research Centre, Oxford University and the Centre for the Philosophy of Natural and Social Sciences, London School of Economics. Thanks also go to Brasenose College, where William Petty, a founding father of national income measurement, was once a fellow, for hosting the meeting in which our most recent survey was finalized.

Intended for a variety of readers, this overview draws on a large body of research strewn across a number of scientific disciplines. There are inevitably many researchers whose work I regret not having had the space to discuss (more) but I hope that this overview both provides a useful road map of an expanding field that matters to us all and helps to underline the fact that we can indeed now measure and understand economic progress in terms of human wellbeing and happiness. Further material can be found at www.happinessexplained.org.

SELECTED BIBLIOGRAPHY

Ackerman JM, Kenrick DT, and Schaffer M (2007) Is friendship akin to kinship? *Evolutionary Human Behavior*, 28, 365–74

Adams R and Blieszner R (1995) Aging well with friends and family, *American Behavioral Scientist*, 39, 209–16

Alonso and 29 other authors (2011) Days out of role due to common physical and mental conditions: results from the WHO world mental health surveys, *Molecular Psychiatry*, 16, 1234–46

Alpizar F, Carlsson and Johansson-Stenman O (2001) How much do we care about absolute versus relative income and consumption? Goteborg University, Department of Economics

Anand P (1993) *Foundations of Rational Choice Under Risk*, Oxford: Oxford University Press

Anand P, Durand M, and Heckman J (2011) The measurement of progress—some achievements and challenges, *Journal of the Royal Statistical Society: Series A*, 174(4), 852–5

Anand P, Gray A, Liberini F, Smith R, and Thomas R (2015) Wellbeing over 50, *Journal of Economics of Ageing*, available online 18 March 2016

Anand P, Hunter G, Carter I, Dowding K, Guala F, and van Hees M (2009) The development of capability indicators, *Journal of Human Development and Capabilities*, 10(1), 125–52

Anand P, Krishnakumar J, and Tran NB (2011) Measuring welfare: Latent variable models for happiness and capabilities in the presence of unobservable heterogeneity. *Journal of Public Economics*, 95(3), 205–15

Anand P and Roope L (2014) The development and happiness of very young children, Open and Oxford Universities, mimeo

Anand S and Sen A (1994) *Human development index: methodology and measurement* (No. HDOCPA-1994-02). Human Development Report Office (HDRO), United Nations Development Programme (UNDP)

Anderson ES (1999) What is the point of equality? *Ethics*, 109, 287–337

Anderson G, Leo TW, and Anand P (2014) Multi-Dimensional Wellbeing Assessment: A General Method for Index Construction with an Application to Multivariate Deprivation Measurement, mimeo, University of Toronto

Argyle M (2001) *The Psychology of Happiness*, London: Routledge

Armstrong MI, Birnie-Lefcovitch S, and Ungar MT (2005) Pathways between social support, family well being, quality of parenting and child resilience: what we know, *Journal of Child and Family Studies*, 14, 269–81

Arneson RJ (1999) Human flourishing versus desire satisfaction, *Social Philosophy and Policy*, 16, 1–48

Ashida S, Wilkinson AV, and Koehly LM (2012) Social influence and motivation to change health behaviors among Mexican origin adults: implications for diet and physical activity, *American Journal of Health Promotion*, 26(3), 176–9

Aslam, A and Corrado L (2012) The geography of well-being, *Journal of Economic Geography*, 12, 627–49

Australian Government (2013) *Capability Review*, Review Report, September Canberra, Austalia

Bache I and Reardon L (2013) An idea whose time has come? Explaining the rise of well-being in British politics, *Political Studies*, 61, 898–914

Bache I, Reardon L, and Anand P (2015) Wellbeing as a wicked problem: navigating the arguments for the role of government, *Journal of Happiness Studies*, published online 28 February

Back MD, Schmukle SC, and Egloff B (2008) Becoming friends by chance, *Psychological Science*, 19, 439–40

Bagwell CL, Bender SE, Andreassi CL, Kinoshita TL, Montarello SA, and Muller JG (2005) Friendship quality and perceived relationship changes predict psychosocial adjustment in early adulthood. *Journal of Social and Personal Relationships*, 22, 235–54

Baker-Henningham H and Lopez Boo F (2010) Early childhood stimulation interventions in developing countries, IZA discussion paper 5282

Banerjee A, Deaton A, and Duflo E (2004) Health, health care and economic development, *American Economic Review*, 94, 326–30

Baranowski T, O'Connor T, Hughes S, Sleddens E, Beltran A, Frankel L, Medoza JA, and Baranowski J (2013) Houston . . . we have a problem! Measurement of parenting, *Childhood Obesity*, 9, S1–4

Baron RA and Markman GD (2000) Beyond social capital: how social skills can enhance entrepreneurs' success, *Academy of Management Executive*, 14, 106–15

Bartram D (2011) Economic migration and happiness: Comparing immigrants' and natives' happiness gains from income. *Social Indicators Research*, 103(1), 57–76.

Bates W (2009) Gross national happiness, *Asian-Pacific Economic Literature*, 23(2), 1–16 (online)

Baumard N, Andre J-B, and Baumard N (2013) A mutualistic approach to morality: the evolution of fairness by partner choice, *Behavioral and Brain Sciences*, 36, 59–122

Baumeister RF, Catanese KR, and Vohs KD (2001) Is there a gender difference in strength of sex drive? Theoretical views conceptual distinctions and a review of relevant evidence, *Personality and Social Psychology Review*, 5, 242–73

Beath J and FitzRoy F (2007) Status happiness and relative income, IZA discussion paper 2658

Beauchamp MH and Anderson V (2010) SOCIAL: An integrative framework for the development of social skills, *Psychological Bulletin*, 136, 39–64

Bel G, Fageda X, and Warner ME (2010) Is private production of public services cheaper than public production? A meta-regression analysis of solid waste and water services, *Journal of Policy Analysis and Management*, 29, 553–77

Bellini S (undated) Making (and keeping) friends: a model for social skills instruction, POAC

Berndt TJ (1992) Friendship and friend's influence in adolescence, *Current Directions in Psychological Science*, 1, 156–9

Berndt TJ (2002) Friendship quality and social development, *Current directions in Psychological Science*, 11, 7–10

Binder M and Coad A (2011) From Average Joe's happiness to Miserable Jane and Cheerful John: using quantile regressions to analyze the full subjective well-being distribution. *Journal of Economic Behavior & Organization*, 79(3), 275–90

Binswanger M (2006) Why does income growth fail to make us happier? Searching for the treadmills behind the paradox of happiness, *Journal of Socio-Economics*, 35, 366–81

Birditt KS and Anonucci TC (2007) Relationship quality profiles and wellbeing among married adults, *Journal of Family Psychology*, 21, 595–604

Biswas-Diener R, Vitterso J, and Diener E (2005) Most people are pretty happy, but there is cultural variation: the Inughuit, the Amish and the Massai, *Journal of Happiness Studies*, 6, 205–26

Bjarnason T, Bendtsen P, Arnarsson AM, Borup I, Iannotti RJ, Lofstdet P, Haapasalo I, and Niclasen B (2012) Life satisfaction among children in different family structures: a comparative study of 36 Western Societies, *Children and Society*, 26, 51–62

Blanchflower DG and Oswald AJ (2004) Well-being over time in Britain and the USA, *Journal of Public Economics*, 88, 1359–86

Blau ZS (1961) Structural constraints on friendships in old age, *American Sociological Review*, 26(3), 429–39

Bleichrodt, H and Quiggin J (2013) Capabilities as menus: a non-welfarist basis for QALY evaluation, *Journal of Health Economics*, 32, 128–37

Bleske-Rechek AL and Buss DM (2001) Opposite-sex friendship: sex differences and similarities in initiation, selection and dissolution, PSPB, 27, 1310–23

Bolton GE and Ockenfels A (2000) A theory of equity, reciprocity and competition, *American Economic Review*, 90, 166–93

Bradford WD and Dolan P (2010) Getting used to it: the adaptive global utility model, *Journal of Health Economics*, 29, 811–20

Bradshaw J, Keung A, Rees G, and Goswami H (2011) Children's subjective well-being; international comparative perspectives, *Children and Youth Services Review*, 33, 548–56

Braverman P, Egerter S, and Williams DR (2011) The social determinants of health: coming of age, *Annual Review of Public Health*, 32, 381–98

Brereton F, Clinch JP, and Ferreira S (2008) Happiness, geography and the environment, *Ecological Economics*, 65(2), 386–96

Brum F and Palmer C (2002) 'Opportunity structures: urban landscape, social capital and health promotion in Australia, *Health Promotion International*, 17, 351–61

Bruni L and Stanca L (2005) Income aspirations, television and happiness: evidence from the world values surveys, Universita degli Studi di Milano, Dipartimento di Economia Politica

Bryan LC and Gast DL (2000) Teaching on-task and on-schedule behaviors to high-functioning children with autism via picture activity schedules, *Journal of Autism and Development Disorders*, 30, 553–67

Calero C, Gonzales V, Soares Y, Kluve J, and Corseuil CH (2014) Can arts-based interventions enhance labour market earnings among youth? Evidence from a randomised trial, Inter-American Development Bank

Cappelen AW, Moene KO, Sorensen EO, and Tungodden B (2013) Needs versus entitlements—an international fairness experiment, *Journal of the European Economic Association*, 11, 574–98

Carbery J and Buhrmester D (1998) Friendship and need fulfilment during three phases of young adulthood, *Journal of Social and Personal Relationships*, 15, 393–409

Cason TN and Mui VL (1998) Social influence in the sequential dictator game, *Journal of Mathematical Psychology*, 42, 248–65

Chalss N, Guth W, and Miettine T (2009) Beyond procedural equity and reciprocity, Jena Economic Research Papers

Chetty R, Hendren N, Kline P, Saez E, and Turner N (2014) Is the United States still a land of opportunity? Recent trends in intergenerational mobility, NBER working paper series No 19844

Ciarrochi J, Kashdan TB, Leeson P, Heaven P, and Jordan C (2011) On being aware and accepting: A one-year longitudinal study into adolescent well-being *Journal of Adolescence*, 34, 695–703

Clark AE, Georgelllis Y, and Sanfey P (2001) Scarring: the psychological impact of past unemployment, *Economica*, 68, 221–41

Clark AE, Kristensen N, and Westergard-Nielsen N (2009) Economic satisfaction and income rank in small neighbourhoods, *Journal of the European Economic Association*, 7, 519–27

Colquitt JS, Conlon DE, Wesson MJ, Porter OLH, and Ng KY (2001) Justice at the millennium: a meta-analytic review of 25 years of organizational justice research, *Journal of Applied Psychology*, 86, 425–45

Comim F, Qizilbash M, and Alkire S (eds) (2008) *The capability approach: concepts, measures and applications*. Cambridge: Cambridge University Press

Conti G and Heckman J (2012) The economics of child well-being, IZA Discussion Paper 6930

Cunha F, Heckman JJ, and Schennach SM (2010) Estimating the technology of cognitive and non-cognitive skill formation, *Econometrica*, 78(3), 883–931

Currie J (2004) Child research comes of age, Department of Economics, UCLA

Dassopoulos A, Batson CD, Futrell R, and Brents BG (2012) Neighborhood connections, physical disorder, and neighbourhood satisfaction in Las Vegas, *Urban Affairs Review*, 48, 571–600

Deaton A (2008) Income, health and wellbeing around the world: evidence from the Gallup World Poll, *Journal of Economic Perspectives*, 22, 53–72

Demir M, Jaafar J, Bilyk N, and Ariff MRM (2012) Social skills, friendship and happiness: a cross cultural investigation, 152, 379–85

Dercon S and Sanchez A (2013) Height in mid childhood and psychosocial competences in late childhood: evidence from four developing countries, *Economics and Human Biology*, 11, 426–32

DeScioli P and Kurzban R (2009) The alliance hypothesis for human friendship, PLOS ONE, 4(6), e5802, 3 June

Diekmann A (2004) The power of reciprocity: fairness reciprocity and stakes in variants of the dictator game, *Journal of Conflict Resolution*, 48, 487–505

Dolan P, Peasgood T, and White M (2008) Do we really know what makes us happy? A review of the economic literature on the factors associated with subjective well-being. *Journal of Economic Psychology*, 29(1), 94–122

Drobnic S, Beham B, and Prag P (2010) Good job, good life? Working conditions and quality of life in Europe, *Social Indicator Research*, 90, 205–25

Duckworth AL, Peterson C, Matthews MD, and Kelly DR, (2007) Grit: perseverance and passion for long-term goals, *Journal of Personality and Social Psychology*, 92, 1087–101

Dufwenberg M, Gachter S, and Hennig-Schmidt H (2011) The framing of games and the psychology of play, *Games and Economic Behavior*, 73, 459–78

Durlak JA, Weissberg RP, and Pachan M (2010) A meta-analysis of after school programs that seek to promote personal and social skills in children and adolescents, *American Journal of Community Psychology*, 45, 294–309

Dush CMK, Taylor MG, and Kroeger RA (2008) Marital happiness and psychological well-being across the life course, *Family Relations*, 57, online public access

Easterlin RA (2001) Income and happiness: towards a unified theory, *Economic Journal*, 111, 465–84

Easterlin RA (2006) Life cycle happiness and its sources: intersections of psychology, economics and demography, *Journal of Economic Psychology*, 27, 463–82

Eiser C and Morse R (2001) Can parents rate their child's health-related quality of life? Results of a systematic review, *Quality of Life Research*, 10, 347–57

Ekins P, Dresner S, and Dahlstrom K (2008) The four-capital method of sustainable development evaluation, *European Environment*, 18, 63–80

Engle PL, Black MM, Behrman JR, Cabral de Mello M, Gertler PJ, Kapiriri L...and Young ME (2007) Strategies to avoid the loss of developmental potential in more than 200 million children in the developing world, *The Lancet*, 369(9557), 229–42

English Longitudinal Survey of Aging, www.elsa-project.ac.uk

Erdil E and Yetkiner IH (undated) A panel data approach for income-health causality, Middle East Technical University, Department of Economics

Faggian A, Olfert MR, and Partridge MD (2011) Inferring regional well-being from individual revealed preferences: the 'voting with your feet' approach, *Cambridge Journal of Regions, Economy and Society*, 5, 163–80

Falk A, Fehr E, and Fischbacher U (2007) Testing theories of fairness—intentions matter, *Games and Economic Behavior*, 62, 287–303

Fan CS, Wei X, and Zhang J (2005) 'Soft' skills, 'Hard' skills, and the Black/White Earnings Gap, IZA Discussion paper 1804

Fave AD, Brdar I, Freire T, Vella-Brodrick D, and Wissing MP (2011) The eudaimonic and hedonic components of happiness: qualitative and quantitative findings, *Social Indicators Research*, 100, 185–207

Fedderke J, Kadt RD, and Luis J (1999) Economic growth and social capital: a critical reflection, *Theory and Society*, 28, 709–45

Fehr E and Schmidt KM (1999) A theory of fairness, competition and co-operation, *Quarterly Journal of Economics*, 114, 817–68

Feldman MA (1994) Parenting education for parents with intellectual disabilities: a review of outcome studies, *Research in Developmental Disabilities*, 15, 299–332

Finkelstein A, Luttmer EFP, and Notowidigdo MJ (2012) What good is wealth without health? The effect of health on the marginal utility of consumption, *Journal of the European Economic Association*, 11, 221–58

Fioraravanti CH (2012) Brazilian fitness programme registers health benefits, *The Lancet*, 380, 206

Fleurbaey M (2012) *Fairness, responsibility, and welfare*, Oxford: Oxford University Press

Flouri E and Buchanan A (2002) What predicts good relations with parents in adolescence and partners in adult life: findings from the 1958 British birth cohort, *Journal of Family Psychology*, 16, 186–98

Forsythe R, Horowitz JL, Savin NE, and Sefton M (1994) Fairness in simple bargaining experiments, *Games and Economic Behavior*, 6, 347–69

Fredrickson BL (2006) How eudaimonic and hedonic motives relate to the well-being of close others, *Journal of Positive Psychology*, 1, 57–9

Frey BS, Benz M, and Stutzer A (2004) Introducing procedural utility: not only what but also how matters, *Journal of Institutional and Theoretical Economics*, 160, 377–401

Frey BS and Stutzer A (2012) The use of happiness research for public policy, *Social Choice and Welfare*, 38(4), 659–74

Friel S and Marmot MG (2011) Action on the social determinants of health and health inequalities goes global, *Annual Review of Public Health*, 32, 225–36

Frijters P and Beatton T (2012) The mystery of the U-shaped relationship between happiness and age, *Journal of Economic Behavior and Organization*, 82, 525–42

Fujiwara D (2013) A general method for valuing non-market goods using well-being data, Centre for Economic Performance, Discussion paper 1233

Furnham A and Brewin CR (1990) Personality and happiness, *Personality and individual differences*, 11, 1093–6

Galambos CM (1998) Preserving end-of-life autonomy: the patient self-determination act and the uniform health care decisions act, *Health and Social Work*, 23, 275–81

Gibbons S and Olmo S (2011) School quality, child wellbeing and parents' satisfaction, *Economics of Education Review*, 30, 312–31

Glaeser EL, Laibson DI, Scheinkman JA, and Soutter CL (2000) Measuring trust, *Quarterly Journal of Economics*, 115(3), 811–46

Glenn ND and Weaver CN (1981) The contribution of marital happiness to global happiness, *Journal of Marriage and the Family*, 43, 161–8

Graham C (2005) The economics of happiness. *World Economics*, 6(3), 41–55

Graham C (2009) *Happiness around the world: The paradox of happy peasants and miserable millionaires*. Oxford: Oxford University Press

Guth W and Tietz R (1990) Ultimatum bargaining behaviour, *Journal of Economic Psychology*, 11, 417–49

Hamalainen TJ and Michaelson J (2014) *Wellbeing and Beyond*, Cheltenham: Edward Elgar

Hanushek EA and Luque JA (2003) Efficiency and equity in schools around the world, *Economics of Education Review*, 22, 481–502

Harker K (2001) Immigrant generation, assimilation and adolescent psychological well-being, *Social Forces*, 79, 969–1004

Heady B, Muffels R, and Wagner GG (2010) Long-running German panel survey shows that personal and economic choices, not just genes, matter for happiness, *PNAS*, 107(42), 17922–6

Health Canada (2001) *Fairness in Families Schools and Workplaces*, Minister of Public Works and Government Services

Healy M (2011) Should we take the friendships of children seriously? *Journal of Moral Education*, 40, 441–6

Heckman JJ and Kautz T (2012) Hard evidence on soft skills, *Labour Economics*, 19, 451–64

Heide Avd, Delines L, Faisst K, Nilstun T, Norup M, Paci E, Wal Gvd, Masss PJ vd on behalf of the EURELD consortium (2003) End-of-life decision-making in six European countries: descriptive study, *The Lancet* 362, 345–50

Helliwell JF (2003) How's life? Combining individual and national variables to explain subjective well-being, *Economic Modelling*, 20, 331–60

Hick R (2011) The capability approach: insights for a new poverty focus, *Journal of Social Policy*, 40(2), 291–308

Hoffman E and Spitzer ML (1985) Entitlements, rights and fairness: an experimental examination of subjects' conceptions of distributive justice

Hoffmann JP and Ireland TO (2004) Strain and opportunity structures, *Journal of Quantitative Criminology*, 20, 263–92

Howard C (2010) Are we being served? A critical perspective on Canada's Citizens First satisfaction surveys, *International Review of Administrative Sciences*, 76, 65–83

Hudson E (2013) Does relative material wealth matter for child and adolescent life satisfaction? *Journal of Socio-Economics*, 46, 38–47

Humphrey SE, Nahrgang JD, and Morgeson FP (2007) Integrating motivational, social and contextual work design features: a meta-analytic summary and theoretical extension of the work design literature, *Journal of Applied Psychology*, 92, 1332–56

Huppert FA (2009) Psychological wellbeing: evidence regarding its causes and consequences, *Applied Psychology: Health and Wellbeing*, 1(2), 137–64

Huta V, Pelletier LG, Baxter D, and Thompson A (2012) How eudaimonic and hedonic motives relate to the well-being of close others, *Journal of Positive Psychology*, 7, 399–404

Ibarra H and Hunter M (2007) How leaders create and use networks, *Harvard Business Review*, 85(1), 2–8

Jim CY and Chen WY (2010) External effects of neighbourhood parks and landscape elements on high-rise residential value, *Land Use Policy*, 27, 662–70

John K (2001) Measuring children's social functioning, *Child Psychology and Psychiatry Review*, 6, 181–8

Johnson AJ (2001) Examining the maintenance of friendships: are there differences between geographically close and long-distance friends? *Communication Quarterly*, 49, 424–35

Johri R (2005) Work values and the quality of employment: a literature review, Department of Labour, New Zealand Government

Jones CI and Klenow PJ (2010) Beyond GDP? Welfare across countries and time, NBER working paper 16352

Joyce K, Pabayo R, Critchely JA, and Bambra C (2010) Flexible working conditions and their effects on employee health and wellbeing, Cochrane database of systematic reviews, Art no.: CD008009

Kaplan SN, Klebanov MM, and Sorensen M (2008) Which CEO characteristics and abilities matter? University of Chicago Graduate School of Business, mimeo

Keefer P and Khemani S (2005) Democracy, public expenditures, and the poor: understanding political incentives for providing public services, *World Bank Research Observer*, 20, 1–27

Kingdon GG and Knight J (2007) Subjective well-being poverty vs. Income poverty and capabilities poverty? *Journal of Development Studies*, 42, 1199–224

Kittle B, Paetzel F, and Traub S (2013) Who cares about equity? A social norm revisited, Department of Economic Sociology, University of Vienna

Klugman J, Rodriguez F, and Choi H-J (2011) The HDI 2010: new controversies, old critiques, *Journal of Economic Inequality*, 9, 249–88

Knabe A and Ratzel S (2011) Scarring of scaring? The psychological impact of past unemployment and future employment risk, *Economica*, 78, 283–93

Knack S and Keefer P (1997) Does social capital have an economic payoff? A cross-country investigation, *Quarterly Journal of Economics*, 112, 1251–88

Krugman PR (1987) Is free trade passé? *Economic Perspectives*, 1, 131–44

Larson RW and Verma S (1999) How children and adolescents spend time across the world: work play and developmental opportunities, *Psychological Bulletin* 125, 701–36

Leventhal T and Brooks-Gunn J (2000) The neighborhoods they live in: the effects of neighbourhood residence on child and adolescent outcomes, *Psychological Bulletin*, 126, 309–37

Liberini F, Proto E, and Redoano, M (2013) Happy voters, Department of Economics, Warwick University, mimeo

Lin N and Dean A (1984) Social support and depression: a panel study, *Social Psychiatry*, 19, 83–91

Lloyd KM and Auld CJ (2002) The role of leisure in determining quality of life: issues of content and measurement, *Social Indicators Research*, 57, 43–71

Lovejoy K, Handy S, and Mokhtarian P (2010) Neighborhood satisfaction in suburban versus traditional environments: an evaluation of contributing characteristics in eight California neighborhoods, *Landscape and Urban Planning*, 97, 37–48

Luttmer EFP (2005) Neighbors as negatives: relative earnings and well-being, *Quarterly Journal of Economics*, CXX(1), 963–1002

Lymbomirsky S and King L (2005) The benefits of frequent positive affect: does happiness lead to success? *Psychological Bulletin*, 131, 803–55

Lyons MD, Huebner ES, Hills JK, and Horn MLV (2013) Mechanisms of change in adolescent life satisfaction: a longitudinal analysis, *Journal of School Psychology*, 51, 587–98

Marmaros D and Sacerdote B (2004) How do friendships form? Discussion paper, Google.com and Dartmouth College

McKee-Ryan FM, Song Z, Wanberg CR, and Kinichi AJ (2005) Psychological and physical well-being during unemployment: a meta-analytic study, *Journal of Applied Psychology*, 90, 53–76

Mcquilllin B and Sugden R (2012) Reconciling normative and behavioural economics: the problems to be solved, *Social Choice and Welfare*, 38, 553–67

Meier S (2006) A survey of economic theories and field evidence on pro-social behaviour. Federal Reserve Bank of Boston, Massachusetts

Mejia A, Calam R, and Sanders MR (2012) A review of parenting programs in developing countries: opportunities and challenges for preventing emotional and behavioural difficulties in children, *Clinical Child and Family Psychology Review*, 15, 163–75

Meyer-Bereby Y and Niederle M (2005) Fairness in bargaining, *Journal of Economic Behavior and Organization*, 56, 173–86

Mitra S (2006) The capability approach and disability, *Journal of Disability Policy Studies*, 16, 236–47

Murie A and Musterd S (2004) Social exclusion and opportunity structures in European cities and neighbourhoods, *Urban Studies*, 41, 1441–59

Murnighan JK and Saxon MS (1998) Ultimatum bargaining by children and adults, *Journal of Economic Psychology*, 19, 415–45

Namazie C and Sanfey P (2001) Happiness and transition: the case of Kyrgyzstan, *Review of Development Economics*, 5, 392–405

Napier JL and Luguri JB (2012) Moral mind-sets: abstract thinking increases a preference for 'individualising' over 'binding' moral foundations, *Social Psychological and Personality Science*, 4, 754–9

Newcomb AF and Bagwell CL (1995) Children's friendship relations: a meta-analytic review, *Psychological Bulletin*, 117, 306–47

Ng SW (2012) Time use and physical activity: a shift away from movement across the globe, *Obesity Reviews*, 13, 659–80

Ng YK (2003) From preference to happiness: towards a more complete welfare economics, *Social Choice and Welfare*, 20, 307–50

Nussbaum M and Sen A (1993) *The quality of life*, Oxford: Oxford University Press

Nussbaum MC (2001) *Women and human development: The capabilities approach* (Vol. 3), Cambridge: Cambridge University Press

Oberle E, Schonert-Reichl AS, and Zumbo BD (2011) Life satisfaction in early adolescence: personal neighbourhood, school, family and peer influences, *Journal of Youth Adolescence*, 40, 889–901

OECD (2011) Compendium of OECD Wellbeing Indicators, Paris

OECD (2013) How's life? Measuring wellbeing. Paris

Offer A (1997) Between the Gift and the Market: The Economy of Regard, *Economic History Review*, 50(3), 450–76

Offer A (2000) Economic Welfare Measurements and Human Well-Being, Discussion Paper, Nuffield College, Oxford

Offer A (2007) *The Challenge of Affluence*, Oxford: Oxford University Press

Orth U, Robins RW, and Widaman KF (2012) Life-span development of self-esteem and its effects on important life outcomes, *Personality Processes and Individual Differences*, 102, 1271–88

Osberg L and Smeeding T (2006) Fair inequality? Attitudes to Pay Differentials, mimeo

Oswald AJ and Wu S (2011) Well-being across America. *Review of Economics and Statistics*, 93(4), 1118–34

Pagliani P (2010) Influence of regional national and sub-national HDRs, Human Development Research Paper

Park N (2004) The role of subjective well-being in positive youth development, *Annals AAPSS*, 591, 25–39

Pattanaik PK (2011) The ethical bases of public policies: a conceptual framework, mimeo Department of Economics, University of California, Riverside

Patterson TL, Goldman S, McKibbin CL, Hughs T, and Jeste DV (2001) UCSD performance-based skills assessment: development of a new measurement of everyday functioning for severely mentally ill adults, *Schizophrenia Bulletin*, 27, 235–45

Persky J (1995) The ethology of *Homo Economicus*, *Journal of Economic Perspectives*, 9, 221–31

Peterson C, Park N, and Seligman MEP (2005) Orientations to happiness and life satisfaction: the full life versus the empty life, *Journal of Happiness Studies*, 6, 25–41

Piketty T (2014) *Capital in the Twenty-First Century*, Cambridge, MA: Belknap Press

Pogge TW (undated) Can the capability approach be justified? mimeo

Pollard EL and Lee PD (2002) Child wellbeing: a systematic review of the literature, *Social Indicators Research*, 61, 59–78

Portes A (1998) Social capital: its origins and applications in modern sociology, *Annual Review of Sociology*, 24, 1–24

Powdthavee N (2007) Economics of happiness: A review of literature and applications, *Chulalongkorn Journal of Economics*, 19, 51–73

Power TG (2013) Parenting dimensions and styles: a brief history and recommendations for future research, *Childhood Obesity*, 9, s14–21

Proctor CL and Linely PA (2009) Youth life satisfaction: a review of the literature, *Journal of Happiness Studies*, 10, 583–630

Putnam RD (1995) Bowling alone: America's declining social capital. *Journal of Democracy*, 6, 68

Rand DG, Tarnita CE, Ohtsuki H, and Nowak MA (2013) Evolution of fairness in the one-shot anonymous ultimatum game, *Proceedings of the National Academies of Sciences*, 110, 2581–6

Ratcliffe A (2010) Housing wealth or economic climate why do house prices matter for well-being? CMPO Working Paper Series 10/234

Rawls J (2009) *A theory of justice*. Harvard: Harvard University Press

Rego A and Cunha MP (2009) Do the opportunities for learning and personal development lead to happiness? It depends on work-family conciliation, *Journal of Occupational Health Psychology*, 14 (3), 334–48

Resnick MD, Harris LJ, and Blum RW (1993) The impact of caring and connectedness on adolescent health and wellbeing, *Journal of Paediatric Child Health*, 29, S3–9

Reyes-Garcia V and Tsimane' Amazonian Panel Study (TAPS) (2012) Happiness in the Amazon: Folk Explanations of Happiness in a Hunter-Horticulturalist Society in the Bolivian Amazon in *Happiness Across Cultures* (eds) Selin H and Davey G, Springer, Dordrecht

Roberts SGB and Dunbar RIM (2011) The costs of family and friends: an 18-month longitudinal study of relationship maintenance and decay, *Evolution and Human Behavior*, 32, 186–97

Robeyns I (2005) The capability approach: a theoretical survey. *Journal of Human Development*, 6(1), 93–117

Robles MM (2012) Executive perceptions of the top 10 soft skills needed in today's workplace, *Business Communication Quarterly*, 75, 453–65

Rook KS (1991) Facilitating friendship formation in late life, *American Journal of Community Psychology*, 19, 103–10

Rose SM (1984) How friendships end: patterns among young adults, *Journal of Social and Personal Relationships*, 1, 267–77

Ryan RM and Deci EL (2001) On happiness and human potentials, *Annual Review of Psychology*, 52, 141–66

Sachs JD (2013) Restoring virtue ethics in the quest for happiness, ch 5 in *World Happiness Report*, New York

Schoeman F (1985) Aristotle on the good of friendship, *Australasian Journal of Philosophy*, 63, 269–82

Schokkaert E (2009) The capabilities approach, in Anand P, Pattanaik P, and Puppe C (eds) *The Handbook of Rational and Social Choice*, Oxford: Oxford University Press ch23

Schotter A, Weiss A, and Zapater I (1996) Fairness and survival in ultimatum and dictatorship games, *Journal of Economic Behavior and Organization*, 31, 37–56

Schultz K (1991) Women's adult development: the importance of friendship, *Journal of Independent Social Work*, 5, 19–30

Schurer S and Yong J (2012) Personality, well-being and the marginal utility of income: what can we learn from random coefficient models, University of York, Working Paper 12/01

Scully D, Kremer J, Meade MM, Graham R, and Dudgeon K (2014) Physical exercise and psychological well being: a critical review, *British Journal of Sports Medicine*, 32, 111–20

Semyonov M, Lewin-Epstein N, and Maskileyson D (2013) Where wealth matters more than health: The wealth-health gradient in 16 countries, *Social Science and Medicine*, 81, 10–17

Sen A (1970) The impossibility of a Paretian liberal, *The Journal of Political Economy*, 78, 152–7

Sen A (1979) Personal utilities and public judgements: or what's wrong with welfare economics, *The Economic Journal*, 89, 537–58

Sen A (1999) *Development as Freedom*. Oxford: Oxford University Press

Sen A (2000) The discipline of cost-benefit analysis. *The Journal of Legal Studies*, 29(S2), 931–52

Sen A, Williams B, and Williams BAO (eds) (1982) *Utilitarianism and beyond*. Cambridge: Cambridge University Press

Sen AK (2003) Missing women—revisited, *British Medical Journal*, 327(7427), 1297–8

Sen AK (2009) *The Idea of Justice*. Harvard: Harvard University Press

Sener IN, Eluru N, and Bhat CR (undated) An analysis of bicyclists and bicycling characteristics: who, why and how much are they bicycling? University of Texas at Austin, mimeo

Seyfarth RM and Cheney DL (2012) The evolutionary origins of friendship, *Annual Review of Psychology*, 63, 153–77

Smith L, Anand P, Benattayallah A, and Hodgson TL (2015) An fMRI investigation of moral cognition in healthcare decision making, *Journal of Neuroscience Psychology and Economics*, 8 (2), 116–33

Stiglitz J, Sen A, and Fitoussi JP (2009) The measurement of economic performance and social progress revisited. *Reflections and overview. Commission on the Measurement of Economic Performance and Social Progress*, Paris

Stutzer A and Frey BS (2010) Recent advances in the economics of individual subjective wellbeing, *Social Research*, 77, 679–714

The Happiness Research Institute (2014) The Happy Danes, Copenhagen

Trapp GSA, Giles-Corti, B, Christian HE, Bulsara M, Timperio AF, McCormack GR, and Villaneuva KP (2014) Increasing Children's Physical Activity: Individual, Social and Environmental Factors Associated with Walking to and from School, *Health Education and Behavior*, 39(2), 172–82

Tyler TR (1988) What is procedural justice? Criteria used by citizens to assess the fairness of legal procedures, *Law and Society Review*, 22, 103–35

UNDP (1990) *Human Development Report*, Oxford: Oxford University Press

Ura K, Alkire S, Zangmos T, and Wangdi K (2012) A short guide to Gross National Happiness Index, Thimpu, Centre for Bhutan Studies

Van der Gaag MP and Snijders TA (2004) Proposals for the measurement of individual social capital, 199–218 in Flap H and Volker B (eds) *Creation and returns of social capital*, London: Routledge, 199–218

Vansieleghem N (2013) What is philosophy for children? From an educational experiment to experimental education, *Educational Philosophy and Theory*, online: Taylor and Francis

Varelius J (2005) Health and autonomy, *Medicine Health Care and Philosophy*, 8, 221–30

Veenhoven R (1991) Is happiness relative? *Social Indicators Research*, 24(1), 1–34

Veenhoven R (2009) How do we assess how happy we are? Tenets, implications, and tenability of three theories, in Dutt AK and Radcliff B (eds) *Happiness Economics and Politics*, Cheltenham, Edward Elgar, ch 3

Verbrugge LM (1977) The structure of adult friend choices, *Social Forces*, 56, 576–97

Volkert J and Schneider F (2011) The application of the capability approach to high-income OECD countries: a preliminary survey, CESifo, Working paper 3364

Walker S and 13 other authors (2011) Inequality in early childhood: risk and protective factors early child development, *The Lancet*, 378, 1325–38

Wallander JL, Schmitt M, and HM Koot (2001) Quality of Life Measurement in Children and Adolescents: Issues, *Instruments and Applications*, 57(4), 571–85

Waller R, Gardner F, Hyde LW, Shaw DS, Dishion TJ, and Wilson MN (2012) Do harsh and positive parenting predict parent reports of deceitful-callous behaviour in early childhood, *Journal of Child Psychology and Psychiatry*, 53, 946–53

Wang H and Wellman B (2010) Social connectivity in America, *American Behavioral Scientist*, 53, 1148–69

Weiss A, King JE, Inoue-Murayama M, Matsuzawa T, and Oswald AJ (2012) Evidence for a midlife crisis in great apes consistent with the U-shape in human well-being, *PNAS*, 109(49), 19949–52

Winkelmann L and Winkelmann R (1998) Why are the unemployed so unhappy? Evidence from panel data, *Economica*, 65, 1–15

Winzelberg GS, Hanson LC, and Tulsky JA (2005) Beyond autonomy: diversifying end-of-life approaches to serve patients and families, *Journal of the American Geriatric Society*, 53, 1046–50

Wolbring T, Keuschnigg M, and Negele E (2013) Needs, comparisons and adaptation: the importance of relative income for life satisfaction, *European Sociological Review*, 29, 86–104

Wolff J (1998) Fairness, respect, and the egalitarian ethos. *Philosophy & Public Affairs*, 27(2), 97–122

Wolff J and De-Shalit A (2013) *Disadvantage*. Oxford: Oxford University Press

Wydick B, Glewwe P, and Rutledge L (2013) Does international child sponsorship work? A six-country study of impacts on adult life outcomes, *Journal of Political Economy*, 121, 393–436

Yamamoto S and Takimoto A (2014) Empathy and fairness: psychological mechanisms for eliciting and maintaining prosociality and co-operation in primates, *Social Justice Research*, 27, 1–35

Yang Y (2008) Social inequalities in happiness in the United States, 1972 to 2004: An age-period-cohort analysis, *American Sociological Review*, 73, 204–26

INDEX

access to services 35–7
accident victims 61–2
Action for Happiness 117
activity 12–14
adolescence 39–40, 48–51, 76–7
age and life satisfaction 65–8
Alderfer, Clayton 71
Aldi 86
Amato, Paul 29–30
Argyle, Michael x, 79
Aristotle vii–viii, 9, 74
Australia 109
autonomy 39–41, 54–6, 82, 85–6, 106, 116, 117
Avenue Q 62

baboons 75, 76
Barro, Robert 68
'battle of the sexes' game 83–4
Beautiful Mind, A 84
Becker, Gary 27, 98
Belk, Russell 69
Bentham, Jeremy 14
Berlin, Isaiah xi
Better Life Compendium, OECD 112–13
Bhutan 103–5
biology and fairness 94–6
Blanchflower, David 66
Bowling, Ann 53
Brickman, Philip 61
Bristol University model of gender inequality 99–100
Brondolo, Elizabeth 101
burnout 81–3

California urban/suburban study 34–5
capuchin monkeys 96
'chicken' game 84–5
childhood/children 39, 43–8, 81–2, 119
child sponsorship programmes 50–1
chimpanzees 75, 76

China 35
communities 33–4, 115–16, 117
community learning 107
Csikszentmihalyi, Mihaly 81
cultural homogeneity 105–6

Danish Commission on Aging 54
Denmark 53–4, 65, 71, 105–6
depression 38, 39, 50, 87, 100
discrimination experience 100–1
divorce 30
domestic violence 32, 97–8
drug/substance abuse 38, 40, 49, 89, 112, 122

Easterlin, Richard 3, 30, 57, 66–7
eating disorders 38, 49
economic (GDP) growth 3–4, 21, 57–8, 62–3, 68, 103
economic/income inequalities 4–5, 60, 62–5, 98, 99
economics of happiness and wellbeing 57–69
education *see* schooling
empathy 94–5
employment *see* work
end of life autonomy 54–6
engagement with life 116–17
Engle, Patrice 47, 48
English Longitudinal Survey of Aging (ELSA) 51–3
English surname study 64
equal opportunities 14, 27, 96, 98–100, 121
eudaimonia vii–viii, x
exercise 39, 86–8
experience 12–14
experience measures 14–16
externalities 3–4
extroversion 30–1, 79

fairness and justice 19, 91–101, 116, 117
families and family life 4, 29–32, 81–2